HOW TO BE A
BOSS
B*TCH

HOW TO BE A
BOSS
B*TCH

Stop Apologizing for Who You Are
and Get the Life You Want

CHRISTINE QUINN
with Rachel Holtzman

ABRAMS IMAGE, NEW YORK

CONTENTS

A TYPICAL TUESDAY

Let me set the scene: It's a gorgeous, sun-soaked day on the Adriatic Sea, somewhere off the coast of Croatia. The temperature is a perfect 80-something degrees, and we're surrounded by glimmering water so stunning that Instagram filters wish they could do it justice #Wanderlust. My husband and I are aboard a three-story, 185-foot yacht with some close friends, celebrating the wrap of *Selling Sunset*'s smash third season. It's first-class all the way, from the 360-degree views to the grand winding staircase to the gold, mirrored foyer that looks like Donatella herself manifested this floating mansion. It's regal, opulent, and completely over the top, but if you've watched even one episode of my hit Netflix series, then you know it's exactly my speed for vacation mode. Fuck, for a Tuesday. We have a full staff, a yoga instructor, Jet Skis, a water trampoline, a three-story slide, and pretty much all the toys at our disposal. It's every overconfident drunk person's best friend—and every Malia from *Below Deck*'s worst nightmare.

I'm sitting on one of the yacht's oversize lambskin couches on the main level, nestled in a chinchilla throw worth more than my first annual salary. Going over my schedule for the day in my signature Louis Vuitton agenda, I pencil in work meetings that I have to arrange, list emails to reply to, and review my research for upcoming interviews I've booked during the trip. Doing a lot of press is normal for me by now; whether I'm at home or on vacation, it never stops. (But then again, neither do I.) First up on my itinerary is a Zoom interview with a reporter from *Vogue*. My publicist arranged the interview to chat about real estate, the show, and my style. The usual. What I don't know at this point is that I'm about to drop a bomb that will change not only my life but other people's lives, too.

I get on the call, and the reporter starts listing all of my accolades in real estate and entertainment. We talk about my experience as a realtor in a male-dominated industry, and how I'm a top producer in my office. I'd recently dominated on multiple listings—one of which was $17 million, the biggest listing for any woman in our office to date—all while filming a top Netflix series six days a week for six months straight.

"I really don't know how you do it all," the reporter says. "You are the definition of a businesswoman."

Suddenly, I'm overcome by a feeling I barely recognize. There's something about the way she's rattling off all these amazing accomplishments that makes me realize that I'm not telling the full story. We continue on with the interview, and I'm doing my best to focus, except this feeling won't go away and now I'm sweating and anxious like I'm back at church. I'm shook in a way that I rarely am—because it only happens when

I'm lying. I think about how the article is going to read, what message I'm sending to people, and realize I can't keep this secret inside any longer.

I stop her mid-sentence. "You know what?" I say. "There's something I want to tell you that I've honestly never told anyone in my entire life other than my immediate family and my husband. Seriously, no one knows."

There's no turning back now.

"I don't have a high school diploma or even a GED. I have an eighth-grade education."

I can hear her struggling to find something to say as I break down crying. I'm breaking down in front of *Vogue*, for chrissake. Even my waterproof Christian Dior Iconic Overcurl mascara is failing me as a stream of black tears line my face. Where I come from, everyone finishes high school and goes on to college. Period. Anyone who strays from that past is an outcast. No, a failure. Add that to my already hard-to-comprehend life, and it makes me a straight-up circus freak. And I've just spelled this out to a reporter whose job it is to share it with the world.

But then a funny thing happens. Within seconds, literally, of making this confession, I feel better. (Though, mental note: Let's not make a habit of doing this!) I feel like a weight has been lifted because for years and years, I'd been lying on resume after resume about my education, hoping that people would give me a chance instead of judging me off the bat. (It's not exactly like being tall, blonde, and big-boobed has people assuming that I'm actually really smart.) And the super fucked-up thing is that I've built a life on authenticity. Whether it's my clients, my friends, my husband, or my fans, they know exactly what they're getting with me because I've realized that to try to be anyone else but me is letting myself down in the end. Here I was preaching about keeping things real and telling it like it is when I'd been carrying around this massive secret. Not only that, I was covering up for something that's pretty much bullshit anyway. I may not have finished school—for reasons I'll get into later—but all those accomplishments that the reporter was oohing and aahing over? That's all me, baby. *I* made that happen, degree or no degree.

But I didn't always see it that way. I was ashamed of what I perceived to be this shortcoming, and because I saw myself as less-than, I let that define me. After years of playing the "dumb blonde" in order to fit into the spaces I thought I needed to squeeze myself into—at work, in relationships—I had begun to think that I was that person. But there eventually came a point when I could say *Wait a minute! I'm not perfect. So what?!* I felt it was my duty to let women know, starting with this interview. I wasn't going to let that "imperfection" define me—fuck no. Because I may not have all the right degrees, but you bet your ass I have a PhD in life. And right now, in this moment, I'm about to prove that when it comes to living my truth, I get all the extra credit.

A few weeks later, after I'd left the luxury of the yacht for my Los Angeles home—which, granted, with its infinity pool and closet for my four hundred pairs of Louboutins isn't exactly slumming it—the article came out. It was *everywhere* . . . and then came the flood of messages. I held my breath as I scrolled through the DMs pouring in on Instagram. But instead of calling me dumb or making me feel shame for what I thought for so long was a short-coming, people were *thanking* me. By being honest and owning my shit, I had inspired them that they, too, could achieve great things with a less-than-stellar resume and, even better, made them feel better about their own deep, dark insecurities.

This was a huge turning point for me. Laying it all out for *Vogue* taught me that sharing your whole truth is not about throwing yourself a pity party; it's about re-labeling the parts of you that society wants to slap its own brand on, not giving a fuck about what anyone thinks about it, and soaring even higher because you don't have a bunch of extra baggage weighing you down (no matter how cute it is). I'm not sorry for who I am, where I come from, or who I've become; I'm not apologizing for any of it. Neither should you. And you know what that makes us? A couple of Boss Bitches.

CALL ME YOUR BITCH

Let's get one thing straight right up front: If you're going to call me a bitch, I'm going to take it as a compliment. "Bitch" is just a name people give you when they don't know what to do with you, or you make them uncomfortable, or you push them outside of their comfort zone. It's a word men call strong, assertive women who threaten them, but when women use it, it should be a power word. It's time to change the narrative.

If you're anything like me, people have probably called you a bitch with the intention to label you, use it against you, and hurt you. But when I use the word "bitch," I wear it like a badge of honor where it used to be a scarlet letter. I expect you to do the same. Because no one's ever been called a bitch for being a quiet, amenable woman who never makes any waves. As Eleanor Roosevelt said, well-behaved women rarely make history. Bitches have opinions and they make things happen. So, it's about time we took the word "bitch" back for ourselves. From this page forward, when I say it, I am referring to you, a badass who takes no shit, goes after what she wants, and doesn't apologize for it.

I've always been different and outspoken, and I've never had any trouble telling people No. As a result, I've been categorized as a bitch for most of my life. From my teen years onward, whenever I had an unpopular opinion, or spoke up in a situation that others didn't, boom, the "bitch" label got slapped on me yet again. Particularly after *Selling Sunset* first came out, and I heard that all-too-familiar refrain about myself: "Oh my God, she's such a bitch."

But why? Because I'm saying the things that everyone else is thinking but they don't have the balls to say? Does that really make me a bitch? Or does that just make me good at what I do? I believe that when women are strong and voice their opinions, it's hard for people to know what to do with that. The easiest thing is to label them and move along. I say let's flip the implication that speaking up and being your own person is something negative. There's absolutely nothing wrong with being honest and authentic. But until the world catches up and realizes this along with us, "bitch" is going to be our label. Personally, I'm going to own it, like I own all the labels I wear. (Yes, I whipped my hair over my shoulder when I wrote that, and no, I'm not sorry for it!)

So, when I call you a bitch, know that I mean it as the highest praise, and also as a way to build your confidence and light a fire under your ass so you can stand up for yourself and start getting everything you want out of your life. But I don't just want you to be a bitch. I want you to be a *Boss Bitch*. I want you to turn heads when you walk into a room, own your style, make bank, and never be afraid to speak your mind.

I'm proud of being a Boss Bitch. Like I said, after the first season of *Selling Sunset*, people were so sweet to reach out . . . and call me a "fucking bitch." To that I said, "Thank you!" because to me that meant I was doing something right. People were talking about me, following me, remembering me. Sure, it was a little bit shocking at first that people could be so mean. They didn't all like me, and a lot of them mistook my character on the show for the real Christine Quinn—and they still do. But then I realized: So what? You can't make everybody happy all of the time, so you might as well focus on making yourself happy.

That's all you can control, anyway.

That is the core theme of this book: To be a successful professional in business, and a happy person in life, you can't adhere to what other people think is correct or even appropriate. You can't try to be who other people want you to be. All you can do is be fully, unapologetically yourself—and therein lies your power.

In this book, I want to help you feel that, and be that, and act on it in a hundred little ways that add up to one big life. I'll talk about sex and money, fashion and fame, gossip and gratitude, confidence and consciousness. Whether it's filming *Selling Sunset*, being a top-producing real estate agent, a perfume and makeup mogul, a brand ambassador for companies like Ciaté Cosmetics, Samsung, and ShoeDazzle, or a wife and a mother, I'll be sharing parts of my life with you, but the driving energy here is *you and your transformation*—telling my story so you can write yours, plus my best advice to help you get past your past, create your present, and plan for your future. You can remake your life to suit you by doing more than you're told, refusing to be a victim, becoming radically yourself, aiming high, and never being afraid to fuck some shit up.

Bottom line, this is a nothing-off-limits, in-your-face guide for how to break free of what you think is holding you back and finally own your life in all its eccentric, unique, passionate, and unedited glory. What will they call you when you secure the bag and step into your true Boss Bitch power? Let's find out.

CHAPTER 1

HEY BITCH, GET OFF THE COUCH!

I wrote this book because I wanted to help women step into their power, take control of their lives, and not even fucking flinch if someone calls them a bitch. Because like I said, around here, we wear that word like a badge of honor. We're going to talk about money, sex, career, style, and your personal brand. We're going to make big fucking moves—live bigger, *be* bigger—and dump the apologies in the trash. But before we can do that, you have to be all in. You gotta put on those big-girl La Perlas and be ready to commit to this process. And most importantly, you have to *believe* that you can make these kinds of changes in your life. I can hear you already saying to yourself, "I could never make that kind of money/dress that way/catch that kind of man/have that kind of career because of excuses A to Z." I know that you're thinking that I somehow had it easier because I was a model or I'm tall and skinny or I have a lot of money. But bitch, let me tell you something: Things were not always 100 for this girl. I did *not* have it easy. I wasn't dealt a good hand early in life—my cards were shit. I've gotten where I am in life because I took the lemons that life handed me and made Clase Azul lemon drops. I didn't do that by whining; I did it with a ton of hard work, relentless hustle, and the confidence that everyone loves a superhero with a gritty backstory.

I know this will come as a shock, but my life was not always Rolexes and Rolls Royces. And what's interesting is that when I first started writing this book, I didn't think that people needed to know that. I honestly thought that my readers would only want to see me living in this pink sparkly world I've created for myself. But then I realized that if we're really going to connect, and if you're really going to trust this process, then I was going to have to step out of my Instagram feed and bare it all—and I'm not talking about my hot-as-hell *Playboy* shoot I did while eight months pregnant. I want for you to know that I haven't always had it all figured out. I was made to feel inadequate and like an outsider because I didn't fit the mold in school; I wasn't always comfortable in my body; I grew up literally trapped in a household ruled by fear; and when it was time to start the big, fabulous life I know I was meant for, I got knocked down. A lot. So, while you may know Marilyn from the show and from my Instagram, now it's time for you to meet Norma Jean.

I'm not sharing these stories because I want you to feel bad for me—because I sure as hell don't feel sorry for myself. No, I want you to hear what I have to say so that you can, once and for all, get past what you might see as obstacles and turn them into your most powerful weapons. I want you to see that no matter how tough things may have been for me, I found a way to keep going and, even more importantly, a way to own that shit. Whatever you want to call it—unfortunate circumstances, bad luck, bad karma, or just a shitty life—that's your past, and the only role it has to play in your life is fuel for your amazing future.

Growing up, the one thing I remember the most was feeling really misunderstood. My parents were incredibly strict, and they believed that if they could hide me away from the world in their protective bubble, then nothing bad would ever happen to me. As a result, my home life was completely suffocating and, at times, felt like prison. I always had to be home at a certain time; when I eventually did make friends, which was not easy for me, I was barely allowed to see them; I was rarely able to watch TV and definitely not allowed to go to the movies; and it was a hard no on fast food or soda. I remember sneaking in cans of Dr Pepper and pretending to cough when I opened them just so my parents couldn't hear it, or whenever we'd be driving down the freeway, telling my parents that I had to pee just as we were passing a McDonald's so that maybe we could go in. Basically, I was told No constantly.

Part of this had to do with my parents' religious beliefs—we were at church every Sunday—and their thinking that the world was a dangerous, corrupt place. Even from the time I was little, I could tell that my parents let fear run their lives and make their decisions for them. But some of it had to do with the fact that my mother, for as long as I can remember, had been surrounded by illness and death. She saw her twenty-one-year-old perfectly healthy brother die of leukemia. Her father died of Parkinson's. She herself had lupus, Raynaud's syndrome, and rheumatoid arthritis so bad that her fingers had fused together. She'd also survived breast cancer twice, needing a double mastectomy by the time she was forty. At one point, when I was in eighth grade, we thought she wasn't going to make it. We'd been swimming when she started having intense pains in her back and was rushed to the hospital. She had a pulmonary embolism, which came out of nowhere and was a freak occurrence, and she needed spinal surgery as a result (and would eventually need open-heart surgery, which she had in 2020). The doctors didn't know whether she would survive the procedure, so we were told to say goodbye.

When I got older, and especially after I became a mom, I realized that her protectiveness was all coming from a good place and that she was just trying to protect me the best way she knew how. And seeing her so ill ultimately gave me the powerful perspective that in life, you never know what the next day will bring—and that the next day isn't even guaranteed. It made me so grateful for my health, which is definitely not a given, and also fueled my drive and persistence. Watching my mom fight every day to just live at times is what gave me the strength to be so tough in the face of adversity and setbacks, even when it hurt; and I'll always be grateful for that. But at the time, I was just a young girl who needed someone to be there for her and to support her hopes and dreams.

As much as home was difficult, school was worse. To say that it was never, ever my thing is a vast understatement. Socially, it was a nightmare. Starting in elementary school, I was always getting in trouble because I was constantly goofing around and trying to make people laugh; I was completely off the hook owing to then-undiagnosed ADD. I got labeled the class clown, and no one took me seriously. By high school, it had only gotten worse. I was loud and silly and would burp in class because I didn't give a shit. People already thought I was the weird girl, so what did it matter if I let my freak flag fly? The popular girls didn't want to hang out with me, and the theater kids didn't think I fit in. I didn't smoke pot, so I wasn't right for the druggy group. I hated being told when I had to be places and do things, so sports were pretty much out for me. And for whatever reason, all the kids thought I was some kind of freak for having a job. Every weekend I'd be at Sonic—the only gig I could get because higher-end restaurants either assumed I was too dumb based on my looks or penalized me for not having high-end restaurant experience on my resume, yet another flaw in the fucked-up system—while the high school kids would hang out in the parking lot ordering smoothies and smoking cigarettes. In my town, none of the kids had to get jobs, so they thought it was lame that I did. I was totally confused why people were so weird about it—I was totally fine making a couple hundred bucks a week that I could buy makeup with. I thought of myself as Hilary Duff in *A Cinderella Story*—so what if I had to work a dreary job; it was just a matter of time before I became the princess I was meant to be. But in the meantime, there just wasn't a group that was a good fit. There wasn't a nice, neat little box for me because that's not the way *I* was.

I could be the loud and silly girl, but I also loved a deep, serious convo. I hated academics, but if something inspired me, I could talk for hours about it—like the solar system, or art. I had a flair for the dramatic and was the ultimate entertainer, but with my homemade or secondhand clothes and absolutely no cultural references whatsoever thanks to the TV detox my parents imposed, I came off as, well, a little weird. I could make connections with some of the kids when I was one-on-one, but when they were in groups, there was no way I could get into those cliques. It was like Lord of the Fucking Flies. I ate lunch in the hallway every day because the cafeteria was this walking gauntlet of people staring at me and being mean, not letting me sit at their table. And even though I knew I was different, and I knew that being different would one day work out for me and help me stand out, it was lonely. So, while my sister was off being a popular girl on the dance squad and the drill team and all those other cool-girl activities, I would spend most of my time at our neighbors' houses watching their dogs. Mainly because I felt like I related better to the animals than I did the other kids.

It didn't help that I was also a complete stranger in my body. I was taller than everyone—boys and girls—and definitely did not feel pretty. I remember this girl, Lindsay, who was super short and petite and cute (ugh, that bitch)—everyone liked her, and I wanted more than anything to be short like her. I spent so much time wishing I could just have another body and resenting the one I had. By the time I was in high school, I started to get the feeling that with my long legs, long torso, and long, blonde hair that people actually liked the way I looked. Except now the girls hated me for it, and the boys only had one way of showing that they were into me, which was by being cruel. (Ever wondered why I didn't end up with Jacob in Season 1? That punk bitch and his friends put gum in my beautiful, long hair in high school and I had to cut it out. You don't get over that.) I suppose it made me feel a touch better to know that people actually envied me, but I could have done without the early lesson in jealousy. Plus, I still wasn't in love with myself. After years of watching my idols Marilyn Monroe and Dolly Parton work their magic on-screen—my favorite hobby was watching old movies on repeat, the perfect escapism—I didn't see their womanly charm in my flat, curveless body. I craved their seductiveness (luscious curves) and wanted the kind of body (rack) that men would want to stare at all day long; we're talking cartoon-style eyes falling out of their heads. Until I could make that happen, I spent more time envying people's bodies than I did learning to love mine.

To make matters worse, I was a terrible fit for the traditional education system. I was formally diagnosed with ADD when I was twelve years old and had a very hard time not assing around long enough to pay attention in class. I would read what we were supposed to be learning in a book, but then it wouldn't translate to my brain. I also had a really hard time with math and memorizing all the abstract equations that might as well be in another language for a visual learner like me. And it took me longer to take tests because I was a total perfectionist. As a result, I got labeled "dumb." I had to be pulled out of my classes to go to the room for the "special" kids who needed an aide or more time to take a test, and it was mortifying. The other kids would make fun of me, and for the longest time I just accepted that I was stupid—and that school was stupid, too. When it came to English and science and creative topics that stoked my creativity and imagination, I was on it. But having to learn the way the system wanted me to learn and about the topics it wanted me to learn about, I was completely checked out. School became an extension of home, with me always being told No. Always being told to "be here, do this"—I could never understand why they could say, "Hey, there's a test on Friday at 10:30 A.M." I didn't know how I was going to be feeling then, or if I was going to be able to focus. My brain just didn't work that way; it needed more flexibility and space to do its thing. I hated feeling so boxed in and like I was always having to follow rules that didn't make any sense to me and didn't seem to serve any purpose—definitely none of mine. And the less I cared, the worse grades I got, and the worse my grades got, the less I cared. Eventually I was failing all my classes because I didn't want to do the work. It didn't seem relevant to me—like seriously, what was I going to do with algebra? In my mind, I just wanted to get school over with so I could go start my real life. And in a twisted way, I got my wish because I got kicked out.

OK, maybe that's a little dramatic, but my parents saw how much I was struggling and decided that my mom would try to homeschool me. That lasted for a few months because ultimately my mom saw that I wasn't getting the work done and she wasn't able to help me because she was too sick. So the only solution left was to enroll me in an "alternative" school. It was one of those programs where you go to class for a few hours a day along with other kids who couldn't make it in the regular school system. We're talking drug dealers, gangbangers, girls who had gotten pregnant at fifteen, girls who got picked up by their pimps at the end of the day, kids who lit fires in their schools or sent other kids to the hospital. But this is what it had come down to; it was the only choice left for me. The plan was that I'd go to my job at Sonic from six A.M. to eleven A.M., then my mom would pick me up and I'd go to school from twelve P.M. to four P.M. Initially, I felt sorry for myself. I didn't relate in any way to these other kids and had a hard time understanding how I got here and how this was my life. I honestly couldn't see how things could get any worse. But then, I got grateful.

Going to this school had made me grow up fast. I mean, I had legit gang members as classmates for fuck's sake. It opened my eyes to the way the world really worked, not the world that my parents had tried to create for me. In the real world, I wasn't a weirdo. I was unique, talented, creative, and vibrant, just like the other kids in class. For the first time, I fit in. Not only did the other kids like me, but pretty quickly after starting school, I fucking ran that place and eventually was voted prom queen for our little version of the ceremony. I made friends and realized that I had more talents than fucking algebra—I was sharp and funny. I also learned that I was artistic, which I got to express when I'd go out tagging with some of the graffiti artists at school. Sure, we were a bunch of misfits, but only because we didn't fit into any one mold—which I now saw was a positive, not a negative. And we may have flunked out of our regular high schools, but my classmates were certified geniuses—these kids were running drug rings at fifteen. I figured out that I wasn't dumb; it was just that school doesn't teach you what you actually need to know in real life. It doesn't prepare you to think of things on the fly or hold your own in an intense situation—things I now knew were my strengths. We knew that we didn't need to memorize a thousand digits of pi or some shit—that's what the calculator on our phones was for. And once I realized that, I wanted to see what other damaging lies I had been trying to make myself believe. Except, before I could do that, I got arrested.

It was my seventeenth birthday, and I had this big plan of skipping classes at the end of the day so I could leave school early and celebrate with some of my school friends at Hooters—something my mom would never let me do, which is why I had to sneak out. I was looking all cute, dressed like a skank because I loved it and because I knew no one would give a shit since school had bigger issues than a coochie hanging out of a skirt. Then, before I could leave for the day, someone came up to me and said, "Hey, I have a birthday present for you." I was like "Great! What is it?" And he slipped a little baggie of weed into my purse. Again, I asked him what it was because it's not like random strangers were slipping things into my purse every day, but all he said was "Happy birthday." My guess was that it was a Valium or something completely mundane, but someone oversaw our little exchange and tattled on me to the on-duty police officer who was stationed at our school.

The guy dragged me into the principal's office and sat me down in front of her. Then came the moment of truth: He said to her, "You have a choice; you can send her to detention, or since she's a legal adult in the state of Texas, you can have her arrested." And do you know what that fucking bitch did? She went with option B. I was brought down to the station, booked with a mugshot, put into a cell, the whole deal. This is the part where you think I'm going to tell you that my parents came right down to pick me up, we all had a good cry, and I swore to forever change my deviant ways. But no. My parents made me sit in that cell for three nights and three days along with prostitutes, violent offenders, and drug dealers. They'd be like "What are you in here for, ho-ing?" And I'd say, "No. I shanked a bitch; leave me alone." We slept, peed, and ate in this one little freezing cold cell while I tried to figure out why my parents wouldn't just come and get me.

I knew that they were trying to teach me a lesson, just in a really messed-up way. But instead of reflecting on my life choices and how I possibly could have prevented this—and I was already scared shitless enough from then on to never fuck with drugs again—I used all that time to take inventory of the things that I wanted to do with my life, and the bullshit that I was completely done with.

At this point, I was coming to terms with the fact that I was done making my life smaller because someone else told me to or living on someone else's terms. I was so tired of not being in control and told No. I realized that the thing I valued most was freedom, and I wasn't going to get that living at home, and I definitely wasn't going to get that hanging around in jail—which, thank fucking God, my friend's mom finally bailed me out of. But that was my "get off the couch" moment. I knew, then and there, that I had waited too long for my life to start. I had a choice sitting in that jail cell: I could have fallen for the sob story that I was some kind of piece of shit who couldn't get her life together—the story that people were trying to write about my life—or I could use all of this frustration and angst to power my transformation, to move me forward. Well, let me tell you, I wasn't about to let a bunch of people who didn't even know the real me dictate my storyline. This became a major theme in my life and served me very well when it came to *Selling Sunset*: The Christine narrative is not up for grabs. Only I get to decide how my story goes, not some producer, not some writer, and definitely not some other chick. We'll talk much more about this exceptionally important lesson later in the book, but for now, let's just say that this nugget of wisdom has served me extremely well, especially in this pivotal moment. I also realized that it didn't matter if up until now my life didn't look Instagram perfect or that I had more baggage than a Real Housewife going to Salt Lake City. I was going to take all these incredible lessons dressed up as faux problems, pack 'em up into my 2001 gunmetal gray Ford Focus with a million and one miles, and get the fuck out.

There was just the small issue of actually leaving because I knew that if my parents found out, they would literally lock all the doors. So one weekend, when they went on their weekly shopping trip to Costco and I knew they would be away for at least two hours, I thought, *Aha, this is my escape!* In those two hours I found an apartment online in Dallas for $400 a month, packed up my car, and drove the thirty miles to freedom. When they came home, they were like "Where's Christine?" I wish I could have seen their faces! They would ask me when I was coming back, and I was like "I'm not. I'm not. I'm not."

Up next was figuring out what I wanted to do with my life now that I had all this hard-earned independence. If I was like everyone else in my grade, I would be thinking about college. But there was no way I was going down that path. School had been such a waste of time where I didn't learn one damn thing, except maybe how nasty people can be for no reason and how I never ever wanted to make anyone feel that way. (Yeah, I know people will say, "Oh, but you're such a bitch on the show"—but I'm a bitch with a purpose. I'm not just a bitch to be a bitch. As my good friends will tell you, if I'm being a bitch to you, it's probably because you deserve it.)

So anyway, college. I could never understand how in high school we basically just get taught these four boxes: English, math, science, and history. Even though there are so many other more interesting, life-applicable boxes! And if you don't check those boxes or get certain grades, then society tells you that you're nothing and that you're never going to do anything with your life. That's fucked up! And if you do manage to make it through the high-school meat grinder, then you take those four boxes and go to another school, pay a shit ton of money to be there, pick another thirty boxes, and then that's your life sentence. Hard pass.

It was strange watching people my age go off to college, and when everyone would ask, "Where are you going to school?" it would be a little awkward, but I didn't feel any pressure to go. Even my parents, who coupon-clipped their way through life and still gladly paid for my sister to go to college, knew that they'd only be throwing their money away if they sent me.

Instead, I was going to enroll in acting classes and live my dream of being a model and an actress. To this day I'm grateful for that decision. Was my life more difficult than all my friends who spent Mommy and Daddy's money getting fancy degrees that they barely use? Fucking right it was. I look at those kids now and so many of them are still in the same place in their lives, but I graduated from the school of hard knocks magna cum laude. I spent that time surviving and grinding and making my own way, which made me a lot stronger and lot more savvy. I say if you're not going to be a doctor or a lawyer, just lie on your resume! Jk. But most of my friends who are creatives and super successful in their areas of expertise agree that there was no need for that degree.

There was only one hitch: If I wanted to get a decent-paying job to cover rent and utilities while I went to acting school, then I kinda did need that degree since I had no other experience besides Sonic and Taco Bell—and the fast-food life was not for me, unless it's eating it in my sugar daddy's Bentley, which is another story for another chapter. I think we can all agree that it's a bullshit system that requires you to have experience in order to get a job, but yet getting a job is the only way to get experience. So lame. But there I was, getting turned down time, after time, after time for jobs that I was, frankly, way too good for. They all wanted to see a degree or experience or both. Or worse, they took one look at my tall, blonde self and decided that I "wasn't a right fit" (aka too stupid to take a drink order). Well, fuck that shit. I was tired of people not giving me a chance. So I reached into my bag of tricks and pulled out a lesson my dad once taught me when I was super nervous to perform in a middle school play: Fake it 'til you make it (Boss Bitch Lesson #487, which you'll learn all about in chapter 4).

In order to put an end to the resume haters and judgy ass-holes once and for all, I doctored my resume. I figured that if I was going to stretch the truth, then I was going for goddamn gold. College: The Juilliard School. I mean, if you're going to dream big, dream big. I didn't necessarily believe that I needed to go to the best performing arts school in the world in order to make it as an actress, but if people were going to play the dumb game of requiring a college degree, then checkmate. I also made up a bunch of references, listed my mom's friends' phone numbers, and got to work looking for a job. Sure enough, right out of the gate I was hired as a bartender. I'd never made a drink in my life—I mean, I'd enjoyed quite a few in my day and loved some good Sex on the Beach . . . but, obviously, not the same. I was, once again, going to have to bend the truth. I went online and studied everything I could about being a bartender and memorized the entire drink menu, plus all the recipes. That's right, bitches—down to the last Manhattan and Mai Tai. I wasn't able to do that in school because I felt so disconnected from what we were learning and knew I'd never once reach for any of it in real life. But once I was passionate about something and saw how it could get me where I wanted to go, this brain of mine kicked into high gear. And after I started the job, I realized that I was really good at it. I could keep all the orders straight in my head while bantering with the customers about their day, listening as they spilled their hearts out and whined about their wife problems. People told me that I was good with advice and that I was smart for my age. It completely validated what I already knew—I wasn't stupid or an undesirable. I was just different, and that was going to help me to stand out.

* * *

I brought that confidence with me as I started my career in modeling. I grew up wanting to be a model because I'd always been captivated by the cover girls I'd see on the magazines in the grocery store or in CVS when I'd go in to shoplift coal black Wet n Wild eyeliner. I'd stare at them, drinking in their clothes and their cool, wondering how someone even got on the cover of a magazine. I was the kid who was always really into makeup and trying to give anyone who I ever had a playdate with a makeover (until I gave one girl a haircut and she wasn't allowed to play with me anymore), I was obsessed with fashion, and I'd also fallen in love with the idea of being in front of the camera from all the afternoons I spent watching old movies. Plus, I was tall and naturally very thin. Modeling seemed like the perfect combination for me—like the ideal end to my Cinderella story. Here I was, emerging from being locked away from the world with nothing but secondhand, homemade rags to my name, about to shine the way I was meant to.

I started seeking out jobs, and it turned out that I was a natural on set. I booked a gig with JCPenney and did a lot of commercial print work, but I'd oftentimes work for free as an extra just to get my picture taken by photographers whose work I admired. One night I was at this studio until like three A.M. because we were getting so many great shots and I didn't want to stop. I was driving home, and a cop pulled me over because he assumed I must have been drunk or on drugs since it was the middle of the night. He insisted on searching my car, even after I explained that I was coming home from a photo shoot. He couldn't understand why I'd be out so late doing that, but I just had so much dedication and drive because it was something I genuinely loved.

* * *

As much fun as I was having, though, I didn't want to keep working for free. And I wanted bigger, more exciting jobs than jumping around in fake leaves in a twinset and khakis. I wanted to get into the luxury market, maybe even high fashion. Honestly, I wanted people to know my name. Up until this point, I'd submitted my headshots to *the* modeling agency in Dallas, the Kim Dawson Agency, over and over again with the hope of finally getting representation, which I knew would take my career to the next level. But every time that I sent my photos, I got turned down. And like I said, this wasn't just one or two times. Most girls in my position would have packed up and gone home. They would have assumed that all this rejection meant that this kind of work just wasn't right for them, or that they weren't cut out for it. I saw it happen so many times, girls who were up for the same jobs as me and would slowly disappear from the casting calls as soon as doors started closing in their face. But not me. In the case of this agency, I thought, *They're only seeing pictures of me; they don't really know the real me or my personality. I have something that all those other pretty girls don't have. Fuck this shit.*

I decided that if I was going to stand out and win them over, then I couldn't wait for them to come to me. So I went to them. I marched into the Kim Dawson Agency office with my headshots—I had made up my mind that I wasn't going to leave until I had some answers, ideally one that wasn't No.

I told the girl at the front desk that I needed to speak with Kim. She was like "Um, who are you?"

I just repeated, "I need to speak with Kim."

The girl was clearly getting flustered and said, "She's in a meeting; who are you again?"

I held my ground and once again said, "She's in a meeting? OK! I'll wait. I need to speak with Kim."

I sat in that damn lobby for what felt like hours until Kim got back to her office. The girl as the front desk grudgingly told me that I could go in, and I knew this was my one shot. I said to her, "Look, I wanted to give you the chance to meet the person behind these photos and to see that I'm so much more than just a face on a piece of paper. I know you see hundreds of girls, but I've got something that those pretty girls don't. Please just give me a chance." And you know what? She did. She was impressed by my drive (hey, some people call it being a stalker psycho, some call it tenacity). And yes, she was really into the fact that I wasn't just like all the other girls she'd met with in her office. My face was one thing, but my unique personality was what set me apart.

Right out of the gate she booked me in a major runway show for Dallas Fashion Week with an amazing designer named Oscar Fierro, who made these incredible gowns. He was this 5'5" spicy spitfire of a man who was way beyond his time, booking beautifully diverse models for his shows—Black girls, curvy girls, trans girls. He explained to me that he chose models not because of how they looked but because of their energy and their passion. He would praise us for our walk and our turns, and he was always hyping us up, but he never said anything about our bodies; the work was never physical or superficial in that way. I loved modeling because of the feeling that it gave me, and this confirmed that performing wasn't about showing off my body or my face; it was purely an energetic exchange. It made me feel so powerful and comfortable in my own skin, which I'd never felt before. I was goddamn Kanye walking the runway.

After that show, Oscar took me under his wing, like the gay dad that I never had. He went on to book me in every single one of his shows, and when I did my first shoot for *Vogue*, it was in one of his dresses. He was truly the first person who believed in me, the first person who told me that I was incredible and that anything was possible. It was the first time I knew that someone genuinely understood me, and it gave me the best feeling in the world: Like I could do anything if I put my mind to it. And best of all, like I was finally free to live the life that I knew that I'd be able to build once I left behind the doubters and the haters.

Meanwhile, I was also starting out as an actress. The second I got out of high school, I had enrolled in acting classes. It was the very first thing I did because I knew in my bones that acting was what I was meant to do. Some kids know they're going to grow up to be a doctor or a veterinarian or an astronaut or whatever, but I didn't ever lie awake at night knowing that acting would be my life's purpose. What I did know was that I wanted to entertain people. I'd always loved being the class clown, making dumb jokes, making people laugh—I craved the attention, and I felt inspired by the creativity of coming up with new material. Plus, I loved the escapism of a good performance. I could be anyone, anywhere. It was a way for me to prove that there was so much more to me than people saw. I wasn't just the blonde idiot; I could play all kinds of characters with so much more depth. I'd stand in front of the mirror and mimic the performances I'd seen in movies, matching their cadence and tone and pauses. I could deliver their lines to a T, and I could cry on a dime. After so many years of being told that I wasn't good at anything, this was something that I knew I could nail.

In one of these classes I met Tony. He was a misfit, just like me. As a gay man who grew up in the church and lived in such a conservative place, he knew what it was like to be different and to not fit the template of what society said we needed to be. Even though I was eighteen and he was forty-two, we became best friends. Everyone thought it was weird, namely because of our big age difference, but we didn't give a fuck about what anyone said. He was my world, and we made each other the best versions of ourselves. He was my biggest cheerleader as I started going out on auditions, which I did every chance that I could get. I didn't care if it was just a cheesy locally broadcast commercial where my only line was "The pain in my tooth used to send me through the roof!" or if I was an extra with zero lines—I wanted all the experience I could get. At the time, there were tax incentives for the studios to shoot TV shows and movies in Texas, along with Louisiana and Atlanta, so I'd drive as long as it took, sometimes up to eight hours, in that piece-of-shit Ford Focus that would break down every five seconds just to get in front of casting agents and directors. I didn't care if I was just standing around the background or didn't get paid (both of which would happen); I was having the time of my life living my dream of being an actress. I remember my first one-line role and I was like "I get to talk, what?!" It was so cool to me.

But eventually the novelty wore off. The only roles I was getting asked to audition for were "cheerleader" or dumb blonde or "bimbo." I'd completely nail the audition, and yet somehow, I wouldn't get the job. As I said, I knew I was an amazing actor, and I'd always show up prepared, but it felt as if I was constantly being rejected. I'd be like "It literally says that you're looking for someone 5'9" with blue eyes and blonde hair. What the actual fuck?" And they'd tell me that the person who got the role was the director's niece or the best boy grip's mother's sister's cousin's nanny. It made me realize that no matter how talented I was, I was still going to have to figure out how to set myself apart. There were all these people out there who were getting a leg up purely because of who they knew. I wasn't naive; I knew that getting ahead had a lot to do with your connections, but I didn't necessarily think that my lack of cachet would hold me back when I was way more talented than these other girls. I knew I was going to have to get creative in order to stand out. I started being more intentional with how I could get people to remember me after an audition, making excuses to talk with the director or convincing them to let me run the lines again and again all different ways, just to make sure they got one take that was exactly what they wanted. I knew that they were seeing five hundred faces a day, and I needed to find ways for them to see that mine had so much more personality behind it. I knew that if they could realize that, then there was no way they would turn me down.

Finally, one day I got the call that I was up for a part in a movie called *Shark Night 3D*, the biggest project I'd ever auditioned for by far. Once again, I drove for eight hours just to get there. I walked in, did my audition, and they're like "OK, thank you so much, appreciate it." Like most auditions, it had gone quickly—me running a few lines with the casting director while the director and a few of his people looked on. I wasn't up for a lead role, so the lines were pretty minimal. In order to stretch my time a little, I kept pushing to do my lines another way, just to give them some variety. Finally, the director said, "Well, if you want to, you can pretend that you're getting eaten by a shark." Well, he was totally kidding, but I'm like *I'm fucking doing it*. This was my chance to get creative and stand out. Right then and there, I got down on the floor and started flailing and screaming with real tears coming out of my eyes. In my acting class, this was called "method acting," and *that's* what got me the job. The director remembered that girl, the girl who acted as if she was getting eaten alive by a shark on the floor of an office conference room. And even more importantly, he knew that she fucking wanted it.

It was my big break. And not only did I have some major screen time in a feature-length film but my face on a billboard on Sunset Boulevard. So what if I died in the first five minutes?

But that definitely wasn't the end of the fairy tale; not even close. Sure, I was starting to make a living on my own terms and I had freed myself from a lot of the limited mindset garbage that I'd been brainwashed with growing up. But I still wanted more for myself and was frustrated that the glossy, glamorous, soul-satisfying life that I was dreaming about still felt like it was at arm's reach. I'd had a whirlwind relationship with an older man who introduced me to some of life's finest things (we'll call him Mr. Valentino, and let's just say there are many more juicy details to come later in this book), and it was like I'd tasted the forbidden fruit. Suddenly, my world seemed way too small. And if there was one thing I couldn't deal with, it was feeling caged in and controlled. It seemed like there was nothing left to accomplish in Dallas, which is when I knew that if I was going to take my life to the next level, then I was going to have to move to Los Angeles.

I got a cute little apartment, found a manager who believed in me and my career, and it seemed like the stars were finally going to align for me to catch my big break. But guess what? It didn't happen. Not even close. I went to every single audition I could, but every role was, once again, for "dumb ho" or "dumb bimbo." Or I'd finally get a break and book something really solid, work my ass off on set along with all the other actors for this legitimate and professional role I'd scored, only to have my screen time reduced to a sex scene. To make it worse, when I asked my (male) agent what the hell happened—because I had only agreed to the nudity in exchange for this really great part on this huge show—he basically just shrugged and told me to get over it because I got paid. I felt objectified and used, and completely disgusted by this system that treated women like interchangeable bodies. Am I asking for you to feel sorry for me because I was tall, skinny, blonde, and pretty? No. But would it have been nice if just one person could have seen past my exterior? Hell yeah. I had proven to myself that I had more to offer the world, but for some reason no one else was buying it. So, after two years of taking on minor, shitty roles that reduced me to a sex object, I realized that if I had any shot of building my dream life, then I was going to have to change things up.

Once again, I'd reached a point in my life where I had two choices: I could go home with my tail between my legs and admit defeat, or I could dig deep and find another way to reach my goals. I sure as hell wasn't going to go back to Texas—especially not after my dramatic exit—so I had one thing left to do: Say to the Universe, "Bitch, if you're going to slam shut so many doors, the least you can do is open a fucking window." And she did. Or in my case, it was another billboard.

After putting acting on the back burner, I decided to give real estate a try. I completely fell into my element. I could essentially be my own boss and had the freedom to make my own hours, the houses were flossy, and once I hit my stride, the money was amazing. I was great at making connections with new people, which meant that I quickly filled up my client roster with names straight out of the Who's Who in LA playbook. And my real-life savvy made me a natural for all of the wheeling and dealing. As much as real estate checked most of my boxes, though, it didn't scratch the itch that acting did. I still wanted to perform. But what I realized was that there was no character currently out there that I really wanted to play. And not only that, I'd been told so many times that I was only cut out for a limited set of characters that were out there. Which told me one thing: I'd need to come up with my own character. And the one that I wanted to play the most was myself. I wished I could be on TV or star in a movie while just being me. It was a far-flung fantasy, I knew, but every night while I was doing my manifestation work (real-life magic that I'll be teaching you all about in chapter 7), I'd include this goal.

Well, every year the Oppenheim Group does a photo shoot of all the agents and has it turned into a billboard on Sunset Plaza. One day Adam DiVello, the creator of *The Hills*, is driving down Sunset, sees the billboard, and is like *Is this for fucking real?* I get it—it's a bunch of hot chicks dressed super cute and we're modeling for . . . a real estate brokerage? So Adam approached Jason and his brother Brett and asked them about doing a show. We all met to discuss it, and initially, I was the only one on board. It took a lot of convincing, but eventually everyone got on board and we went for it. I had no way of knowing what to expect, but I did realize that this was it; this was my moment to make it work for me, as me. It was everything I had been manifesting since I was a little girl.

Five seasons and three million Instagram followers later, I've turned the show into the life I've always dreamed of. I didn't just show up for my scenes and then let Jesus and Netflix take the wheel; I worked my fucking ass off playing the game, spending entire days filming for weeks on end, making binge-worthy drama, and building a platform that opened doors for tons of high-profile collaborations, brand ambassadorships, and beauty product lines—all of which we'll be unpacking throughout this book. The bottom line is this: There were so many times when I was knocked down and I could have gone home, pulled on some sweats, gotten tits deep in a pint of Ben & Jerry's while hate scrolling everyone I went to high school with. I could have gone back to the safety and familiarity of Texas. I could have complained to everyone I came across about how life just isn't fair, or that if only I had more money, more connections, a better family name, or a fancier college degree I would have had more luck. Where would that have gotten me? Not one inch closer to living the life I wanted to live or being the person I knew I was meant to be. So no, I didn't quit. I pushed, shoved, scraped, and clawed my way through and up using all of the Boss Bitch lessons that I'm going to teach you in this book.

I know a lot of people who resent that they had to work so hard to get where they are. But I'm grateful for the hustle. I'm grateful that I wasn't handed anything because it made me who I am and it's gotten me where I am. Take my friend Amanda, the closest friend I had growing up. She also understood what it meant to be an outsider. Plus, our moms were friends, so she was the only person my mom trusted to be hanging out with me. Well, Amanda was fucking loaded. Her dad was the CEO of RadioShack—we're talking built that shit from the ground up; literally created the slogan "You've got questions, we've got answers." And as a result, he was rolling in cash. Their house was straight out of *Dynasty*, and I wished every day that I had been born Fallon Carrington. They were first to get the brand-new BMW Z3. Amanda always had anything she could ever want—I mean, bitch had a water bed before water beds were cool. Like what fifteen-year-old had a water bed?! She had Louis Vuitton purses on purses on purses and tons of clothes and shoes. She was given everything she could possibly want. She went on to go to college, did that whole thing; then had a first-class ticket to do anything she wanted, wherever she wanted, without having to lift a finger for any of it. And when she grew up, want to know what she decided to do? Wait tables. Don't get me wrong—I don't think waiting tables is beneath *anybody*. But that girl could have accomplished amazing things with the kind of resources that she had. There are people who would kill for that kind of privilege. In my opinion, her parents gave her everything except for the most important possessions that money can't buy: Hustle. Ambition. Drive.

I definitely felt differently when I was fifteen, but as an adult, I'm grateful that I wasn't given everything that I ever wanted because it shaped me into the strong, determined person that I am today. I don't know if I would have worked as hard if I'd had that kind of safety net. I grew up with the very real knowledge of how high the stakes can be if you don't succeed. I knew that this country can be the most wonderful place to live, or it can be the most cruel if you can't make your rent or afford healthcare. Because there's zero safety net. Either you succeed, or you fail.

My husband, Christian, and I are always saying how we don't want baby Christian to be raised with a silver spoon in his mouth, and the fucking hilarious thing is that people are literally sending us silver spoons from Tiffany's. But I know that the greatest gift I can give him is the understanding of what it means to work hard. I say this now—and feel free to hold me to it—but I want him to learn the tough life lessons and feel the burn in the belly that comes with needing to do whatever it takes to get where he wants to go. Those things don't come with an Amex Black Card. They grow out of necessity. They grow out of knowing that if you want something in your life to happen, then you need to do whatever it takes to get there. That includes writing your own rule book, which for me is what you're reading at this very moment. Because trust me, if you let someone else write the rules and follow someone else's agenda, the life you end up with is not going to be the one you want.

The best example of this is a guy named Bradley, the big man on campus at my new high school. He was the alpha that boys wanted to be and the girls wanted to be with; he was the prom king to my queen. He and I grew up with identical circumstances—we were equal in so many ways. The same questionable education, the same limited financial situation, the same soul suck of a small hometown. We lost touch after high school, but after the first season of *Selling Sunset* aired—about fifteen years after I graduated—the principal messaged me on Instagram. She was like "I can't believe it's you; I'm so proud of you; with everything you've overcome, I can't believe how much you've achieved." And all I'm thinking is *Thanks for putting me in jail, bitch*, but I played nice instead. I decided to ask her about Bradley since I was genuinely curious about what had happened to him. He had such a magnetism, I thought for sure he'd be like me, living in some big city, enjoying a big life that he built with his street smarts and quick wit. Unfortunately, that wasn't the case. It turns out that he's in jail for drug possession. My heart sank when I heard that—not only because that's not what I would wish on anyone but also because he had so much potential. And it was a stark reminder that something similar so easily could have happened to me. The path he took was pretty much the only one on offer if I had stuck around—working shitty jobs, believing that I wasn't meant for anything more. But something in me knew that I had to do everything it took to find a new path, even if it meant bushwhacking my way through the Amazon jungle of life to carve it out.

* * *

All of this is to say that you might look at my life and think that I had something handed to me along the way. But that most definitely was not the case. I worked my ass off for everything that I have. I made up my mind a long time ago that I wasn't going to be the girl that someone else wanted me to be, and that I was willing to fight for nothing less than amazing. I got my ass off that couch, no matter how shitty my circumstances might have been, and made my own magic.

I've had low points more recently, too, like when I didn't have the fantasy pregnancy, birth, and postpartum that I had been planning on. I won't unpack this part of my life just yet, but basically I was completely blindsided by all the negativity people threw at me when my baby bump didn't look the way they thought it should; an emergency C-section in place of the lavender-scented, candlelit Earth Mama pushing my baby out on a cloud delivery that I thought I'd get; and postpartum depression in place of the sweet, snuggly newborn phase that I thought comes with being a mommy. And even after all of that I was still dealing with people coming at me about how I somehow wasn't up to their expectations of what or how a mom should be—and that was on top of all the bitchiness from the show.

DON'T LET LIFE BE THE BIGGER BITCH

Well guess what? *Life's* a bitch, but we have to do it anyway. Not only that, you have to be the bigger, badder bitch. Persevering and pushing through is always worth it because, no matter how cliché it sounds, things always get better. OK, maybe they'll get worse before they get better, but there's nothing that some hustle, grind, and manifestation can't improve. The universe exists in a balance—light and dark, warm and cold, sun and moon, yin and yang, good and bad, me and Chrishell—you get the idea. When bad things happen, they will eventually be balanced by good things—if you're determined enough to make those good things happen. And not only that, those "bad" things are actually lessons in disguise. All the wisdom and perspective that I've gained in my life came from the obstacles and setbacks. I didn't let the hard shit knock me down—fuck no! I pushed back, and I pushed back harder. Until eventually, all the speed bumps became my personal amusement park. So I truly believe that every low point will show you what you're made of, and give you the chance to be something more. And if I could get where I wanted to be—starring in a hit show, running my own companies, living in multimillion-dollar homes all over the world, cruising the Adriatic Sea on a Tuesday—then you can get where you want to go, too. But to do that, you have to stop feeling sorry for yourself and get off the damn couch.

<u>GET BITCHY</u>

Throughout this book, you're going to learn some of my favorite lessons for living your best Boss Bitch life. And to help you implement these teachings, I've sprinkled in some "Get Bitchy" exercises to put them into motion. I'm not trying to dampen the vibes with homework—though I love a good naughty teacher moment—but I do think it's important to take a moment to really let these lessons sink in and to start to connect your brain and your heart with the life you want. Becoming a Boss Bitch is all about mindset—the more you can change your outlook, the more you'll see the rest of your life start to change. Taking a beat to do these exercises is the most effective way to nudge that needle. Plus, I've always believed that putting pen to paper is a super powerful catalyst, more than just meditating on things or saying you're going to do something. The act of writing things down starts to rewire your brain, until you're able to see the Boss Bitch Matrix for yourself.

For this lesson, I want you to understand that nothing is permanent. Not even a Sharpie—a Mr. Clean Magic Eraser can kick that pen's ass any day. Think about that—if the gold standard of long-lasting permanence isn't even real, what does that mean for your past? As much as you think people might care about you and your business, no one's writing your life story in magic marker. Believe me, they care way too much about themselves to notice what might be happening on your side of the fence. No matter where you've been, what you've done, your fuckups, your accomplishments, tragic fashion choices, poor relationship decisions, getting fired, getting divorced, losing everything—it doesn't matter. That's because you always hold the Mr. Clean Magic Eraser in your hand. It's always there to lift away whatever mistakes you may have made, the life you thought you had to live, or the person you thought you had to be.

Now I want you to think about one of the low points of your life. Really stare at it. Get all up in its business. What was so bad about it? How did it make you feel? How did it affect your life? Now that it's over, what if you took your Magic Eraser and started to dull it around the edges? Could you look at it in your rearview mirror instead of through your windshield? I want you to start to retell that story to yourself, but this time, take ownership of it. Think about the lessons that it taught you, or how it might have made you stronger. Maybe it'll prevent you from making more poor decisions, or motivate you to make necessary changes in your life. Whatever your answers are, write them down and revisit them any time you feel yourself gravitating toward that couch.

CHAPTER 2

THE FIVE BOSS BITCH LANGUAGES

This might come as a surprise, but the first step toward becoming a Boss Bitch isn't throwing on a pair of your red bottoms, marching into your supervisor's office, telling him to fuck off, then strutting your way to your new and improved life. I mean, if that's what your goal ultimately is—get it, girl. But instead of jumping into the deep end, we first need to do a little baby bitch bootcamp. That starts with digging into the deep stuff—as in, what do you value? What do you *want*? You need to get clear on what is most important to you in life so that you can tailor your goals, your work, and your relationships to protect those values. We're talking motherfucking haute couture, bitch, because once you know how to do that, then there's no limit to the power that you wield.

We all value different things in life; that's part of what makes us who we are. For me, it's freedom. From the time I was fifteen, I've been walking away from jobs, people, and situations in which someone was trying to control me because I'm just not happy unless I'm the HBIC.

But maybe independence isn't your thing. For some people, it's more about emotional connection. For some, it's straight-up wealth; for others it is power or reputation. Maybe you're a true hedonist and it's pleasure, or you're adventurous and it's mind-blowing life experiences. Whatever it is, it's the key to unlocking your greatest, most authentic desires. That's why I developed what I like to call the Five Boss Bitch Languages, or Boss Bitch archetypes. There's the Diva Boss Bitch, Undercover Boss Bitch, Matriarch Boss Bitch, Creative Boss Bitch, and Executive Boss Bitch.

Every single person I've known has fit into at least one category. Call me the bitch whisperer, but it's true. I know we're all unique, special snowflakes, but we all have more in common than we think, beginning with our bitch style. By taking this quiz, you'll be able to figure out which one you are and apply the results throughout this book in order to build your new life plan.

So it's time to channel your inner Cher Horowitz with your pink feather pen and answer the questions in the quiz below. Don't worry, it'll be simple and fun—what, did you think I'd be making you do algebra in the second chapter? Get to know me. And get to work.

WHAT KIND OF BOSS BITCH ARE YOU?

For each question, circle the answer that sounds the most like you, even if it's not exact. Consider the spirit of the question more than the details. If you really can't decide between two answers because they both apply to you equally, circle them both. Many Boss Bitches have qualities of more than one type, and that might be you.

1. I love my job because it involves:
   a. Making deals that make it rain.
   b. Making something out of nothing.
   c. Taking care of those with less power than I have.
   d. Being center stage.
   e. Being the puppeteer who holds the strings and controls the marionettes from behind the curtain.

2. The one thing I don't like about my job is:
   a. When people try to tell me how to do my job.
   b. The uninspiring environment.
   c. When someone I'm responsible for gets hurt.
   d. Those rare moments when nobody is paying attention to me.
   e. When somebody calls me out for something (good or bad) I didn't want anyone to know I did.

3. My favorite way to spend the weekend is:
   a. Working.
   b. Getting inspired.
   c. Planning and executing a family activity.
   d. Going to a show (or better yet, being in one).
   e. Taking me time, so I can relax, be alone, and think.

4. My personal style could best be described as:
   a. Boardroom chic.
   b. Boho woodland fairy.
   c. MILF.

d.   Sexy-flamboyant, head-turning.

e.   Classically understated.

5.   **The person I'll most likely fall in love with is:**

a.   Rich and powerful, like me, with business savvy, who looks so sexy in an expensive suit that I can't help imagining taking it off, piece by piece.

b.   A musician, artist, or writer, but not the kind who lives on their parent's couch. The kind who actually makes a living at it and is heartbreakingly talented but not debilitatingly tortured.

c.   My perfect complement, who can do all the things I can't or don't want to do, but won't step on my toes when it comes to running things and will back up my big decisions. They don't complete me because I'm already complete, but they are great at being supportive.

d.   The strong silent type who stands quietly in the background and watches in awe as I steal every show, captivated by my every move. When we get home, we can't keep our hands off each other.

e.   Traditional, kind, and appropriate, but with secret gifts they share only with you. You appear to others to be the perfect couple, but you both know, in the privacy of the bedroom, that there is a lot more complexity (and passion) to your relationship than appearances suggest.

6.   **Here's my take on spirituality:**

a.   I'm all about manifesting success and abundance.

b.   My creative work is my religion, but I'm not saying I'm not inspired by or channeling the energy from some higher power.

c. The whole family attends services together, no argument—but those services could be anything from church to synagogue to mosque to Zen meditation sessions to sitting around the dinner table sharing what inspired us that day. Spirituality takes many forms, but what matters is that the family does it together.

d. Meditation is a much-needed silent space at the beginning and/or end of my day. It helps me keep things in perspective and remember who I am, as I live my fabulous and very public life.

e. I have my own very personal spiritual life I've created and it's nobody's business but mine. I don't talk about it but it's important to me.

7. A true friend:

a. Can banter with me and have a wit as quick as mine but can also chill out and really listen when I need to vent.

b. Gets me and understands (and loves and appreciates) what I do, even when other people don't see my vision.

c. Can sit in my kitchen with me and drink coffee or tea (or wine!) and talk for hours about everything, no matter what's going on around us, including the typical family chaos—screaming kids, barking dogs, whatever, a true friend remains unfazed.

d. Is my number-one fan!

e. Knows how to keep a secret.

8. My biggest fear is:

a. Failing.

b. Being blocked.

c. Being alone.

    d.   Being ignored.

    e.   Speaking in public.

9. My favorite movies, books, or shows are usually about:

    a.   Wealthy or extremely successful people who have to deal with a challenge to their empires, wealth, or reputations, and overcome in the end.

    b.   Artist biopics or anything about the art world, show business, or romantic stories about writers or journalists in foreign countries. Really, if it's about a creative genius, I'm hooked.

    c.   Family dramas. I'm hooked on the dynamics of complex eccentric families.

    d.   Anything with fabulous costumes and beautiful people. Extra points if they sing!

    e.   Mysteries, crime dramas, anything that challenges me to figure out what really happened.

10. My personal motto is:

    a.   Success comes to those who are too busy to go looking for it.

    b.   Do what you love, and the money will follow.

    c.   Nobody loves you like your family loves you.

    d.   You can't teach charisma.

    e.   Stay true in the dark and humble in the spotlight.

RESULTS

Mostly As: You are an EXECUTIVE BOSS BITCH

When it comes to business, you're a savant. You have a sixth sense about what moves to make and you're almost always right (and when you're wrong, you know exactly how to fix it). You're a special type of Boss Bitch because you are front and center in a world still dominated by men, but that doesn't faze you. In fact, you enjoy it and you use it to your advantage. Your business savvy is known and respected at the highest levels of your business, and nobody ever says, "She's good at her job . . . for a woman." (And if they did, they'd get canceled so fast, they'd barely feel you skewering them with your stiletto.) You don't have to brag because your work and considerable success speak for themselves. If you can rock an expensive suit and still look 100 percent woman, if you never get intimidated in a boardroom, if you wear shoulder pads so you can take up all the space you deserve, and if you've smashed every glass ceiling (or plan to) with your Gucci briefcase, you are an Executive Boss Bitch.

Mostly Bs: You are a CREATIVE BOSS BITCH

You have flair, you have style, and your creativity knows no bounds. Maybe you're an artist, a writer, a musician, a chef, a stylist, or a designer. Maybe you're just a genius at putting together an outfit, or you always know what colors work best together, in ways other people never consider. What makes you a Creative Boss Bitch, instead of just a creative, is that you are at, or well on your way to being at, the top of your game. You never let anyone tell you that creativity isn't practical or important because you know it is, and it's exactly what has gotten you to where you are today. Your job might be about creating (whether it's oil paintings or advertising campaigns), or maybe it's what makes you stand out in your usually non-creative profession (it's amazing what can happen when a CFO, a doctor, a lawyer, an accountant, a hospital administrator, or a sales associate applies creativity to the job). Some Creative Boss Bitches are introverts, and that's perfect. You need that alone time to let your creativity ripen and flow before you burst onto the scene with guns blazing. Others are natural front-women for any business and can convince anybody of anything through their creative approaches to any problem. Whatever your personality, a Creative Boss Bitch knows that beauty is truth and that creation in any form is a woman's birthright. That's the secret to her success.

Mostly Cs: You are a MATRIARCH BOSS BITCH

If mama ain't happy, ain't nobody happy. You're the head of the household, the decider, the primary parent, and you run your family like presidents run a country (good ones, anyway). Your purse is stocked with essential items with a precision that puts Navy SEALs to shame. You see all scenarios and can calculate the probability of all possible disasters. Kids love you, men respect you, other women want to be you, and everybody knows not to cross you. Mothering comes naturally, but so does leadership. Nobody tells a Matriarch Boss Bitch what to do because she already knows what to do. You have a fierce, dominant, mother-bear protective instinct, and you've been known to show up in the principal's office to right a wrong done to any child, even if it's not your own. You take your responsibility as a role model seriously so that your girls will grow up to be strong and confident, and your boys will never take advantage of a woman or see them as possessions to control. You practice what you preach, you are wise, and you make everyone around you feel safe, protected, and loved.

Mostly Ds: You Are a DIVA BOSS BITCH

A Diva Boss Bitch makes sure everybody knows she is a Boss Bitch. You are a natural-born performer, on center stage in every aspect of your life. You dress not so much to impress as to make an impression. You revel in your own self-absorption and yet somehow, nobody minds. In fact, they love it. That's because you are charismatic and magnetic. People love to be around you and be like you. Like a moth to a flame, they imitate your style, your mannerisms, and your confidence, but nobody actually feels that unshakable inner confidence quite like a Diva Boss Bitch. You will not be put down, denied, stepped on, or cheated on (you might, for example, trash someone's office if they try it). You know how to get revenge in a big and often very public way, and somehow, you always get away with it. So you like applause? Followers? Compliments and fawning? Sure, who doesn't? But your real secret is that you don't need them because your sense of self is fully intact and you love who you are, unconditionally. Some divas are full of doubt and live for external validation. Not you. You have enough internal validation, but you just happen to enjoy the spotlight, and you know how to keep the fans coming back for more. You are probably photogenic, have a lot of social media followers, and are on some kind of stage for your work, even if it's not a literal stage. The world needs Diva Boss Bitches, not just for entertainment but for inspiration, motivation, aspiration, and to be reminded that women are, and always have been, goddesses.

Mostly Es: You are an UNDERCOVER BOSS BITCH
On the surface, you don't seem like a Boss Bitch. You seem like a very nice person, polite and appropriate, full of forgiveness and empathy. People describe you as compassionate, kind, generous, and courteous . . . but watch out, because if somebody crosses you, they won't get away with it. You won't do something obvious or public like a Diva Boss Bitch would, but even your stealth-mode execution of justice makes it perfectly clear who's

in charge and who won't be pushed around. You are crafty and quick and you have an understated wit that only those closest to you really appreciate. In some ways, you feel like an undercover agent. You like it that not many fully know the real you because it's none of their business who you are. Above all, you are the boss of your life. In your quietly devastating way, you run your own show, with no compulsion to advertise it and no need for anybody to ever question how nice you are. You might live in the Midwest or the South, where being nice is king. But you know what's queen? Being an Undercover Boss Bitch.

MAKE IT A MANTRA

Now that you know what type of Boss Bitch you are, it's time to write yourself a mantra. We'll talk more later about manifestation and how it has the power to create incredible change in your life. But for now, trust me when I tell you that having a mantra, or a statement that you write down and remind yourself of over and over, is actually training your brain to believe in what you want, which in turn makes your thoughts very, very real. We're talking some supreme witchcraft shit right here.

Part of the reason I want you to do this exercise is that right about now your Bitch Boss type might be feeling a little . . . aspirational. You may be able to relate to it, maybe even feel it in your soul, but when it comes to your everyday life, I get that things might feel a little more like Dora the Explorer than Captain Marvel. I mean, you wouldn't be reading this book if you had it all figured out, right? No judgment here.

I want you to go back to what we first talked about in the beginning of this chapter, what you value. Now that you know which Boss Bitch type you are, use that to settle on the motivation that resonates with you—Power? Control? Creativity? Truth? Nurturing? Justice?

Now write down a sentence or two about who you are and what your primary motivation is. I'll go first:

I am a Diva Boss Bitch and I will always find freedom in every area of my life. Opportunities are endless. Money flows to me ten fold. I am happy, healthy, weathy, and loved.

Now your turn—No hesitation. No maybe-laters. No half-assing.

After you've written your own, keep it somewhere that you can see it on a regular basis—taped to your vanity, next to your La Perlas, on the dash of your car, wherever it's sure to be seen so you can repeat it to yourself on the regs. Doing is believing; the future is yours, bitch!

CHAPTER 3

IT COSTS A LOT TO LOOK THIS CHEAP

All credit for this chapter title goes to the fabulous Dolly Parton, who owns her style like nobody else. And not only that, her style works for her—do you think of anyone else when you see sky-high, bleach-blonde hair and a rack of the Gods? That's her trademark, her brand. Believe me honey, that's so much more than just putting clothes on your body. Style *matters*. It's not just how good you are at putting together an outfit—even if you have Jedi styling skills like me—or something you post on social before you change back into your sweatpants (I see you, bitch). According to the official Christine Quinn Guide to Life, style is the *external* expression of your most *internal* self. How's that for some not-so-dumb blonde shit? But seriously, style is how you show the world who you really are. As the incomparable RuPaul would say: "You're born naked and the rest is drag." In his MasterClass—a must-watch in my book—Ru goes on to explain that everything you put on is, in essence, something that was intentionally constructed. Drag doesn't change who you are; it *reveals* who you are. You just have to know yourself, know what works with you, and know what feels right. Bitch, yasss!

The reason this matters is that having your own distinct style gives you a chance to set yourself apart and own who you really are. I live in a city where genetically gifted—err, surgeonetically gifted—people are a dime a dozen. Statuesque runway models roam the streets of West Hollywood like it's some kind of exotic animal preserve. I observe these creatures in their natural habitat: On their morning nonfat, no-foam almond latte runs to Starbucks. These women don't just look like they've stepped straight out of fashion magazines—they *are* straight out of fashion magazines. They are all gorgeous with perfectly spray-tanned skin, Restylane-plumped lips, and freshly Botoxed faces. In a city of so many 10s, how are you ever able to set yourself apart? STYLE.

According to studies at the University of California, 93 percent of our communication is nonverbal. What does that mean? The messages we relay to other people have very little to do with the words that we use. It takes only seven seconds for the human brain to form an impression. So you have only one chance to set yourself apart. Having a distinct approach to what you look like is an opportunity to project a message of confidence, success, seduction, intelligence, warmth, cool—whatever vibe you want people to get from you, style is your language.

Think about it: When people tell you to cover up or dress a certain way, how does that make you feel? Like you're being personally attacked, right? Because it is personal! And most of the time, if someone's trying to fuck with your outside, then it's probably because they're scared of what's on the inside—they're terrified of your power. That's why the most successful people look and dress exactly the way *they* want with *no fear*. They know exactly who they are, and they want the world to know about it. I know that once I learned my style, I refused to let anyone control it—whether it was people around me saying what's right or wrong, or the voice in my head that said I "should" be doing things a certain way. But that didn't happen overnight.

My first vision of my own style came when I was twenty years old. I was working in a bar in Dallas, engaged to a guy who I wasn't sure I'd actually end up marrying (don't worry, I'll give you more of the dirty on that in chapter 6, but for now, let's just call him Mr. Valentino). One day, this gorgeous, well-dressed forty-year-old man with blue eyes and slicked-back blond hair sat down at the bar. He looked me up and down—I was wearing the basic black outfit required of bartenders but had put my own spin on it by wearing a corset with my jeans, and let's be honest, I looked pretty damn good for "dressing to code"—and he uttered hands-down the sexiest thing any man has ever said to me: "You'd look great in a Valentino dress and a pair of Louboutins." How's that for ballsy? And you know what? He was right. When Mr. V said that, something just clicked. What he described was exactly the way I knew I not only wanted, but deserved to dress.

Look at a pair of shoes that someone's wearing down the street, and you can't tell if it's a five-dollar pair or a five-thousand-dollar pair. But you can always tell when they're Louboutins. Their signature cherry-red soles instantly set them apart. You can spot a pair from a mile away. You see those shoes on someone and you fucking know: That bitch is *expensive*. As for Valentino, he's the ultimate Italian designer who knows his way around a woman's body. He makes the kind of classy, gorgeous dresses that, up until that point, I'd only seen on runways. The idea of people owning Valentino, like, having it in their house, was Kim Kardashian-level wild to me at the time. Unachievable. So, of course, I wanted it. I wanted to use my clothes to prove that all the people who doubted me were wrong. Those voices in my head saying, "You're not doing anything," "You're not going anywhere," "Go back to school and get your shit figured out" were silenced when I thought about the power that a Valentino dress and Louboutins had.

After Mr. V made that comment, I told him, "Yeah, well, wouldn't it be nice to afford those clothes?"

His reply: "Why don't I take you shopping?"

Um . . . WHAT?!

"What are you talking about?" I asked him.

"Please, just take me up on this," he said. "Let's go to lunch. Meet me at the mall; we'll have lunch and go shopping."

Obviously, this seemed a little weird to me. But I couldn't resist his offer—I'm all about a free lunch. (I ordered the lobster, of course.) Sure, I wanted to see if he was being serious about the clothes, but he was also this beautiful man, confident and worldly. I had to know more. So as out-there as his offer was, my curiosity (and my desire for those heels) were too strong to resist.

True to his word, Mr. V and I met for lunch, and then he took me shopping. I kid you not, this man spent *tens of thousands of dollars* on clothes and shoes for me—we're talking full-on *Pretty Woman* montage, without the prostitution vibes. I'd been making my own decent-ish living for years by this point, but this kind of money was still unfathomable to me. And then there was the slight issue of me being with someone else at the time . . . But back to the clothes . . .

That shopping spree with Mr. V kicked things off for my developing style and, spoiler alert, our whirlwind relationship. He made me realize that I wanted something more out of my life than my fiancé ever did or could ever offer me. Mr. Going

Nowhere was home drinking Coors Light on the couch while I was dreaming of drinking a flute of Dom while lounging on a Boca do Lobo sofa with Mr. V. He saw something in me, and he wanted to help me get to where he knew I could go, and his first big impact on me was awakening something in me that had been stirring my whole life.

By trying on these incredible clothes, it made me realize how good I could feel in my body. Growing up, I was tall, awkward, and skinny. You know when they say to not trust everything you read online? Well I mean it—websites say I'm 5'7", but girl, I am 5'10". I'm one tall fucking bitch. When I was younger, I hated it. I felt like a string bean, not a woman. It's part of why I always wanted bigger boobs, so I could feel more confident and sexy—like my body could catch up to my brain. After I finally got implants when I was twenty-one years old, I wanted to show off my body more than ever. (As I always say, the higher the tits, the closer to heaven!) I wanted to wear clothes that I felt confident in, clothes that hugged my curves and gave as few fucks as I did. When I would be covered up in a baggy shirt or pants, I didn't feel like I could take on the world. But give me leather and bustiers and it's a different story—hell give me a little butt crack; I didn't care because I wanted it all out on display. I hadn't been born with a body that I loved, but over time I'd learned to, and it was time to unleash just like Britney did after her conservatorship ended, with all the sexy photos.

Fast-forward to a year later when I was in New York my with sugar daddy (Yes, I said sugar daddy. Lets call a spade a spade and not be so damn ashamed of this term!). We were walking down the street when this four-year-old girl came up to me and said, "Mommy! Mommy! It's Barbie!" The woman looked amused, but I said to her, "Honestly, that's the nicest compliment anyone's ever given me." I believed that little girl, that that's what I looked like—her excitement and awe were so genuine. And I loved it. That's when I knew: From now on, Barbie was going to be my patron saint of style.

But my evolution wasn't exactly over yet. After a bit of living like a Barbie girl in my Barbie world, I wanted to push things further. After all, this wasn't just playing dress-up. I saw the power that my newfound style had in my life. It gave me the confidence to quit my bartending job and pursue acting—a big leap for a girl who felt invisible or not good enough for so much of her life. These clothes empowered me to step into what I believed to be my best self and, with it, my best life. I started thinking about the connotations of Barbie, how some people assume she's just another dumb blonde. Hard relate. With my naturally thin body, long legs, and big boobs, that's pretty much all anyone expected of me. But there's an edge to me, too, and twist, a certain *je ne sais quoi*. I'm a lot deeper than people expect me to be, so I wanted to play with that. I thought about dominatrixes, and how sexy and badass they are. They're in control; they know what they want and aren't afraid to dominate their submissives to get it. Since I was a teenager, I'd loved wearing tight pieces, really high boots, and a lot of black. Every time I put on black or red, I just felt sexy. Those are powerful colors to me. I even saw my sister get married in a black wedding dress, which was also really inspiring. (What can I say, great taste runs in the family.) It might sound way too simple, but just by incorporating those colors and dominatrix-inspired accessories into my wardrobe—in addition to my signature pink, fluffy, feathery, bedazzled staples—I started to feel different, and people started treating me differently. It wasn't that people were responding to the clothes necessarily; they were responding to *me wearing the clothes*. Eventually, I realized that this was an expression of myself that was always there. It wasn't about wanting to stand out and be different, it's because I *am* different. Fuck, show me one other girl who can pull off a black wedding dress! The clothes are just a way of letting people know more about the real me and the story that I want to share about myself.

BUILDING YOUR STYLE

As you start to think about what your unique approach to style will be, remember that the number-one rule is to keep it real. Sure, what we wear and how we put ourselves together can be a construct or something that we invent. I mean, I love trying on different personalities with every pair of shoes. (My *Selling Sunset* ice princess alter-ego Svetlana loves her some lime green and hot pink stilettos). But that doesn't mean that this is license to make up a brand-new you. No, your style *is* you, just packaged up all pretty. Or not, if pretty's not your thing. Your style is a way of infusing your own frequency and your own energy into what other people see—with a little bit of magic mixed in.

I truly believe that everyone can find their place when it comes to style, and that's mostly because it isn't just about the clothes you wear. There's a misconception that in order to be stylish you have to have a team of stylists on a monthly retainer. But it's so much more than that. Style is expression. It's a feeling. It's your reputation. It's your confidence. It's the sum total of the way you dress, talk, move your body, or do anything else for that matter. That's why I think the best place to start when defining your style is not in your closet, but in the mirror.

Think about the people you know who have their own signature qualities aside from how they dress. Maybe it's that one friend who's got amazing cleavage, or your coworker who has eyelashes so gorgeous that she looks like a walking Latisse ad. Or the girl at the gym with the beautiful, thick, wavy hair that Rapunzel herself would envy. All of those attributes—whether granted by DNA or by ATM—can be classified as someone's style, especially if you play it up. That's why I like to say that style starts with what's memorable about you.

For me, it's my ass-long, ice-blonde Malibu Barbie hair. And I know that because recently my husband and I were on the run from the German police (looooong story) in the Frankfurt airport, trying to escape to France, and Christian told me to put my hair up since it would be so easy to spot. We're talking total James Bond shit here. As intense as things were at the time, I took it as such a compliment because I really have made a point of playing up that feature in order to define my personal style and make myself memorable.

Now let's do the same thing for you. What's memorable about you? Here's a little exercise that might help: Imagine you were robbing a house. Don't actually rob a house, please (or if you do, don't say that I told you to do it!). If a nosy neighbor was peeking out the window and saw you, how would they describe you to the police? If they saw you in a lineup, what qualities would stand out about you that they'd remember? If it were me, they'd probably be like "It's that tall chick with the long, blonde hair, Victoria's Secret Angel legs, and fabulous nails" (or at least that's what I'd like to think they'd say). What would they say about you? Whatever characteristics immediately come to mind will be the first things to tip you off as you determine your style. If they wouldn't say anything, then we've got some work to do.

GET BITCHY

I love this chapter because it connects back to figuring out what type of Boss Bitch you most identify with. The more you can connect with the core values that light your fire, the clearer sense of self you'll have. And remember what that translates into? Being a Boss Bitch. Pure and simple. So, while it may seem like you're in pursuit of the perfect outside look, you can't perfect that until you're good with what's on the inside. If you have more work to do in the self-love department, then this style challenge will meet you on that level. Or, if you're already on the I'm the Shit tip—and that's the goal—then applying these lessons is a way for you to level up.

To start, I want you to identify your favorite thing about yourself. It should be something that you love, and something that you're always going to have. A sprinkling of freckles across your nose? A luscious pout? An infectious laugh? A killer sense of humor? The way your hair looks beachy and wavy when you let it air-dry? If you need a hint, you could ask a few close friends about what they see as your best quality, physical or not. Or, if there's nothing you can think of that you really like about yourself, then bitch, it's time to take a closer look in the mirror because I know you've got something amazing. Again, it could have nothing to do with the way you look—just something about you that's unique. Once you do find that one special thing, write down the quality or qualities you like best. Then put that note somewhere that you'll see often—ideally the bathroom or closet mirror so you can see it when you're getting ready for the day. Read it to remind yourself to play up that quality, and your personal style will start to shine through.

Another layer to this approach is to think about the elements of style that you already have in place. One little thing about me is that I always wear tons of bracelets on my right wrist (since I'm a lefty). I once noticed that about myself in a photo, and I thought, *Oh, damn, I must really like bracelets.* I'd never really thought about it before, but I always put them on. And they've been part of my signature style ever since. Before you go dismissing this realization as too surface-level, think about what those bracelets represent: Something I like about myself and something that makes me feel good. That right there is pure ego-building, soul-nourishing, self-acceptance-stoking fuel and I'm here for it.

MAKE IT YOUR OWN

I believe that I'm particularly well-qualified to give you this type of advice because I live in Los Angeles, the land of beautiful people. It can't be overstated that everywhere you look, there is a woman who is taller, or has a better body, or a prettier face, or better hair, or whatever else you can imagine (ass, boobs, lips, clavicles, whatever). So, how can anyone who lives in a place like "Lala Land" possibly feel like a beautiful, badass Boss Bitch?

My husband, Christian, explained it perfectly. When we were dating, he said to me, "Everyone in LA looks the same. Everyone's pretty, everyone's this, everyone's that. But you're so much more than that." He told me he fell in love with me for my sense of humor, for my drive, and for everything beneath the surface.

So sweet, right? But also, so true. I'm constantly surrounded by beautiful women, and I'm not going to win in the beauty category. But I know that I can hold a conversation. I can hold my own, and I'm hilarious! Do I ever see these gorgeous women and feel bad about myself? I'd be a narcissist if I told you that I didn't. I absolutely feel that way sometimes. But then I remind myself of everything that I feel confident about, like the way I carry myself, and the unique qualities I have that could never be replicated in another person.

I know you might be rolling your eyes at me right now, me telling you that looks aren't everything. But it's 100 percent true. Back when I was trying to make it in the acting world, there was one woman who I was constantly being compared to when I would go on auditions. I was so jealous of her for the longest time. I had seen all these headshots and pictures of her online and had talked her up in my head. *She's so much prettier than me*, I thought to myself over and over. Which translated to *She's better than me*.

Then I met her in person.

It was like a switch flipped inside my brain. I went from thinking, *She's so much prettier than me* to *Yup, she is pretty, along with thousands of other girls, but she's not me*. She didn't have my spark, my je ne sais qoi, my little somethin' somethin'. If I didn't live in LA, and didn't meet these people as often as I do, I think I'd be totally jaded and jealous of everyone who seems to have it better than me. Comparison SUCKS, end of story. It's not a game anyone can win. If being the Best Looking is your goal, you'll always lose. Sorry, bitches; but that's the cold, hard truth. No matter where you live, or what the people around you look like, there will always be someone better looking, or younger, or with more money to buy designer clothes and accessories. But no one can be you. No one can have your spark, or your style. That's why style matters, and why it's worth your time to hone your own. Plus, we already know that you have great taste since you're reading my book. So now let's work on setting yourself apart.

GET BITCHY

As you identify the ways you love to express yourself and the characteristics that set you apart, go ahead and give your style a name. As you know, I call my personal style "Dominatrix Barbie." That was the result of putting together qualities that made me feel a certain way—over-the-top glam, pink, legs, boobs, dominatrix style, black, red. Take some time to brainstorm descriptors that do the same thing for you. What are colors that make you feel powerful or completely at peace? What articles of clothing do you gravitate toward? Would you never be caught dead in a skirt below the knee, or are you pantsuit girl all the way? Who are style icons you identify with? Are you more Billie Holiday or Billie Eilish? If you're a visual person like me, start pulling together images you find online or in magazines. Go to a fabric store and see what colors and materials speak to you. Go to a store you never dreamed you'd be able to shop in and take pictures of pieces you're in lust with. Then sift through everything you've found and come up with a name for your own iconic style, which will become part of your personal brand. Whether it's ultimately Soccer Mom or Instagram Thot, so long as it rings true to you, there's no wrong answer.

CHAMPAGNE TASTE WITH A COORS LIGHT BUDGET

I think the biggest misconception people have is that "style" is unattainable. Through fifteen-second Instagram and Snapchat stories, we have subconsciously trained our brains to believe that in order to keep up with the Kardashians in the style department we have to have access to an unlimited Amex Black Card or be an A-lister with a glam squad. In some ways, you're right—as we speak, there are teams of stylists curating color-coordinated rolling racks up and down the hallways of museum-inspired Calabasas mansions. But I need you to hear me when I tell you: Style does not equal money. And you also better believe that money does not equal style. Although my closet has enough letter logos to make Sesame Street jealous, I truly don't believe that that's what makes me stylish.

For me, fashion comes from a place of lack. Growing up, my family was poorer than the average family. Which for us meant that my mom would make our clothes. She knew how to sew, so she could inexpensively make us what we needed, especially matching outfits (always with the mommy-and-me matching outfits!). I was never given new clothes as a child, and that bugged me. To the point where it became an obsession. I also had this fabulous aunt, Mary, who was the complete opposite of my mom. Mary was in pharmaceutical sales and was always dating really wealthy men. She had an entire room in her house that was a closet, and I remember thinking, *This is going to be my life*. I may have also thought about how it would be amazing to work over all these men for clothes and bags, but mainly I knew that one day, on my own dime, I would have a room filled with my dream wardrobe.

But I didn't have a sugar daddy—at least not at the time—and I wasn't exactly raking in the cash from Taco Bell and Sonic, so I had to get creative. I started swiping clothes from my sister Alicia, who's five years older than me and ran with a much different crowd. Her cool-girl drill team friends were all super loaded and were always loaning her things from their own closets, which I would alter on my mom's Singer sewing machine. I also quickly learned that I could buy clothes cheap at Ross or TJ Maxx then work my tailoring magic to make them sluttier and shorter and cooler, styling them up, and mixing and matching the pieces to mimic trends I'd see in the magazines at 7-Eleven. And I learned that you can never really tell the difference between a $5 dress and a $500 dress, which gave me confidence that if I did it right, no one would know that I barely had any money in my clothing budget.

I still have the same sense when I style myself now. In fact, I pride myself on it. I'm hella resourceful—let's just say Nordstrom has a killer return policy that I took full advantage of when shooting Season 1, buying and returning dresses for shoot days since I didn't have endless amounts of money. Or I'll put on a $20 dress and pair it with a Rolex, mixing things up, high and low. Or, you know what, fuck the Rolex. Because the accessory that really makes you look expensive is your attitude. If you carry your outfit with confidence, then no one's going to come at you.

BE YOUR OWN ICON

Remember Christina Aguilera back in her chaps, skimpy bras-as-tops, and morning-after makeup days? Coming off the cookie-cutter train of *The Mickey Mouse Club*, she was surrounded by pop culture robots like Jessica Simpson, Mandy Moore, Justin Timberlake, and Willa Ford. These performers played it safe and pleased the big music executives (along with their fans' approving mothers), but not Christina Aguilera. While people applauded Britney Spears's virginity vows, Christina never bothered to deny her sex life, nor defend what really went on backstage at

The Mickey Mouse Club. With murmurs of sex and alcohol behind the scenes, Christina was never one to sugarcoat things. She was ahead of her time in the twenty-first-century feminist movement, so people were definitely not ready when she came out with her sex-positive, dare-to-go-there *Dirrty* video. They were freaking the fuck out, but Christina was like: I don't care. I'm confident enough to love and embrace my sexuality, so take it or leave it. (We'll take it, Xtina!) She was always authentic to who she was, and I respect that. When asked about this iconic cultural moment—which was really like her coming-out party—she said she didn't want to play the pretending-to-be-innocent game. She wanted to be honest and truthful. She called *Drrty* her "fuck-it moment." It was her stepping up, owning her strength and the many forms it took on for her. Is she a Boss Bitch or what?!

The Kardashians also come to mind for me when I think about people with unapologetic style. From day one of *Keeping Up with the Kardashians*, I have always been particularly drawn to Khloé. For me, she was always the "different" one and, as you now know, I can totally relate to feeling that way. But more than that, she would say exactly what she was thinking, popular or not, regardless of whether she thought people would agree. She has continued to set herself apart with her style—I mean, that queen basically invented knee-high boots and hoop earrings. And she's continued to come out on top by staying true to herself and her personal style.

Once you really know who you are, don't be afraid to express yourself with what you wear. This is your official permission—as if you needed it—to really let it fly, whether that means leather chaps (yasss) or something more understated. In style, as in all other areas of your life, make it your own. (Sense a theme yet, bitches?)

* * *

While writing this book, I shared the following quote on Instagram: "The day I changed was the day I stopped trying to fit into a world that never really fit me." I posted it alongside photos of me that were taken while I was filming *Selling Sunset*. I was wearing a hot pink houndstooth-print minidress, a sparkly Gucci barrette, and black sky-high platform Mary Janes. This is actually kind of a big deal because I didn't always have the confidence to dress the way I do at work.

When I first started out in real estate, I had no idea what I was doing. I'll be the first to self-own, and that's what was up—I was clueless, and not in the cute plaid suit and thigh-high way. Since I was coming off working as an actress, I thought about it like playing a part. As in "the role of successful realtor will be played by Christine Quinn." I just needed a costume. Well, you know those real estate mailers you get that feature a woman with her arms crossed over her reasonable, Plain Jane navy or black blazer? That's what I believed I had to wear if I wanted to make it.

I went shopping at Bebe and got myself a rotation of pantsuits and silk camis to mix and match. I spent all this money to look the way I thought I needed to look, even posing for a group photo for the Oppenheim website with my arms crossed over my own black blazer. It was only a matter of time before I had my very own cheesy bench ad. But here's the thing: No matter how hard I tried to convince myself that this was the right thing to do, it didn't feel right. It was SO not me. And feeling uncomfortable and awkward in my clothes did nothing for my confidence. I'd actually taken a step backward, becoming a carbon copy, dime-a-dozen real estate agent with nothing special or unique to offer.

Then, an interesting shift happened. At the time, I was single, and for the first time in a while, I was going out a lot to bars and restaurants to meet new people. When it came up in conversation that I was a real estate agent, I started landing clients. But I wasn't wearing my standard-issue real estate blazer when I did it. No, I was dressed like the real me—boobs to the sky, Made by Mattel-style all the way. *Wait a minute,* I remember thinking. *I'm dressed like a hoochie mama at the bar, and you're telling me that you're trusting me with your listing?* And just like that, it became clear to me: I could be myself and wear what I wanted to and still succeed. In fact, I was succeeding because I was being much more authentic, which translated into more confidence and, well, more *me*. In my real estate flyer outfits, I wasn't telling the truth about who I was. It's why I love when people come at me saying I'm fake—do NOT get this twisted; I am more real and more genuinely me than I ever have been before. Playing dress-up as someone else, on the other hand, was pure counterfeit.

I'd love to tell you that I immediately dropped off all my blazers at Goodwill and started showing up at work in my favorite Hervé Léger dresses. But it was a more gradual change than that. At first, I slid the Bebe blazers off to one side of the closet. Then I started experimenting with outfits that I actually felt good in at work. Day by day, I got the validation that I was moving in the right direction. No one respected me less for being me. In fact, they respected me more. And my business—which is so dependent on making genuine connections with people and developing trust with them—has never been stronger.

Once you've grounded your personal style in who you are and what you stand for, then your capabilities are endless. When you make that connection between how you feel inside and what you look like on the outside, that's a really powerful shift. What you need to realize, though, is that the clothes aren't going to change how people think of you—you wearing those clothes like a boss is what will.

That said, after you've ascended the style ranks and you're feeling yourself harder than Xtina herself, there are people who may come for you—because they always do. That leads me to our next lesson . . .

FUCK THE HATERS

After *Selling Sunset* aired, I'd get comments like "You look like a stripper"—and they didn't mean it as a compliment, even though I took it that way. (Shout-out to all my sex worker bitches who hustle and look good doing it!) And now that I've had a baby, I get even more commentary and hateration about the way I choose to express my style. I've lost count of the number of times I've heard "You're a mom; why are you dressing like that?" What, now that I've given birth it's illegal for me to wear a minidress? I have to shrivel up and move to sweatsuit town? (Though, for the record, I can rock the shit out of a sweatsuit—and you can, too, if that's your speed.) The point is, I refuse to change my style just because I'm a mother now, and I double refuse to allow people to shame me for the way I dress.

No matter how someone comes at me and the way I choose to express myself, I have the same response for them: Thank you! That's right, I thank them. When I walked into the Oppenheim Group office in my fabulous neon green outfit and Heather told me I looked like the Joker, I agreed with her. "Thank you," I said.

"I feel like it!" I don't care what anyone has to say about what I'm wearing. The fact that they're talking about it means I'm doing something right. I don't expect everyone to have taste or to understand me, so I truly don't care what they think. And you shouldn't either. Say "Thank you!" and move on with your (much more fabulous) life.

A friend of mine who worked at a celebrity magazine had a very minimalist style. She wore lots of black—a black tank top layered under a cardigan or jacket was one of her go-to looks—and she always accented her outfits with delicate jewelry. Her boss, the fashion director at the magazine, once gave the staff accessories as gifts, and she chose the simplest of the pieces for my friend. "This one is for you because you're so minimal and simple. Like Jennifer Aniston, with all your plain tank tops." It's unclear whether she meant this as a dig or not (she probably did), but you know what my friend said? "Thank you." If someone is commenting on your style, it's because they noticed it. And that, quite simply, means you're winning.

GET BITCHY

The world is full of haters, we know this. And yeah, we can talk about how to defend ourselves against the nastiest, wartiest Internet trolls. But instead, I want to move beyond that, to the next level of living and being. And on that level, life is aglow with the power of positivity. I'm not getting cheesy on you, I swear. Positivity, especially when you pay it forward, is *suuuper* powerful, especially as you start to feel more comfortable in your own skin. Coming out as a bigger, better, stronger version of you can be scary in the beginning—hell, even when you're a master at it like me. What you need is to feel like there are people who have your back. And the best way to create more positivity in your life is to hand it out yourself and then surround yourself with people who do the same.

I have a really great group of confident women who are my friends, including total rock stars I admire like Khloé Kardashian, Mindy Kaling, Lisa Rinna, and Lilly Ghalichi. We support one another, both in real life and online, writing positive comments on each other's photos. You'd be amazed how a simple *You look amazing!* goes such a long way. In a time when it's so much easier to cut people down, celebrities are often easy targets. The world needs more Khloés and Mindys and the positivity they bring. It's incredibly rare to be a woman in this culture who feels confident in herself and realizes that she's not in competition with anyone else. Let me say that again for you bitches in the back: No one else is your competition. We've all got the same goal: We all just want to stand a little taller, be a little more confident, and feel at home in our own skin. So we need to be lifting each other up, rather than cutting each other down. I want you to practice this in your own life.

Every day for the next week, I want you to pick a woman, online or in real life, and give her a genuine compliment. Maybe she has a great smile or has fabulous shoes or chic sunglasses. Whatever you like about her style, tell her. Repeat this with a new woman each day. Imagine if everyone reading this book took the time to do that, and then the people receiving the compliments paid it forward. Let's go, bitches, we're doing this!

CHAPTER 4

WORK, BITCH

This chapter is *all* about work. Because if there's one environment where every girl I know could use a big shot of Boss Bitch energy, it's in the office. It doesn't matter if you're a hairdresser, a teacher, an ER doctor, or a partner at Big Dick, Big Dick, and Big Dick. It doesn't even matter if you're a stay-at-home mom or someone who is still looking for the job of their dreams. If you have a hustle of any kind, then you need to treat it with the same authenticity and ownership that you do everything else in your life. Because stepping into that power is the secret to success and, ultimately, loving the life you live.

I know this might come as a surprise, coming from the girl with no college degree who's gotten fired (or what I like to think of as mutual parting of ways) from pretty much every job she's ever had since she was a teenager, but I know a thing or two about making it work. The lessons I learned weren't on any fancy B-school syllabus and, honestly, having to scrap and hustle my way from the bottom taught me more about how to fend for myself at the office than any chick will get from Wharton. Fuck, they should pay me to teach a course there . . . can you imagine?! (Seriously, call me.) My approach is a no-fail mix of standing in your power mixed with common sense and a healthy dose of fuck-you attitude—within reason, of course; we're all still professionals. But part of that is knowing when to walk away if something's no longer working for you. And the key to all of this is, that's right, channeling your inner Boss Bitch.

BITCH, STOP APOLOGIZING!

There's this amazing movie called *A Simple Favor*—seriously so good—and it stars Blake Lively and Anna Kendrick. Blake plays this badass B who is also a total fucking sociopath. She meets Anna's character through their kids' school, and Anna's this goofy girl next door who's always stumbling and fumbling and apologizing. Finally, Blake goes, "Never say sorry. It's a fucked-up female habit." Goddamn right!

Why do we women always apologize, especially at work? If you pay attention, you'll notice that almost every woman around you has a habit of saying "sorry." A lot. It's almost like its own punctuation, or an empty word that gets tossed mindlessly into conversation for decoration.

Sorry, but I disagree.

Oh, sorry, I just had something to add.

I'm sorry I didn't respond to this sooner.

Sorry for the long email.

But apologizing all the time isn't you being polite or kind in a way that makes people think more of you. The opposite is true—it minimizes you. It makes you seem less than, like you don't value the way you think or act relative to the people around you. Like you instantly take back anything you're saying that comes after "sorry" because you don't really mean it. Is any of that true? If not, stop acting like it! And if it is, well then, it's extra crucial that you keep reading this book and start being your own best advocate. Because I see you, and I know you're more amazing than this basic-ass shit.

Saying sorry is an example of the people-pleasing that we're trained to do from the time we're little girls. Subconsciously, we think that adding "sorry" whenever we say anything gets us off the hook in case someone disagrees with us. And yes, even dressing the way we think we're supposed to dress and acting the way we think we're supposed to act (bland, submissive) is a form of apology. And trust me, I've been guilty of it, too.

Before I began working with the Oppenheim Group, I was interested in commercial real estate. During one interview, I felt like my potential employer was not only surprised, but also intimidated by the way I was speaking. It was almost unfathomable to this egotistical, over-tanned, dried-up raisin of an executive that a twenty-something-year-old woman was asking and answering all the right questions. And doing so on the same level as his Centrum Silver–popping golf buddies discussing business at their local country club. After all, women my age were usually only on the golf course to serve those men their Arnold Palmers or as arm candy with their asses hanging out of their golf skirts. (Which isn't a look I'm totally down on, but no need to get distracted from the point.) I could tell that he was intimidated by me. He was clueless as to how someone half his age, a woman no less, was speaking to him as an intellectual and professional equal. I apologized in my own way by dumbing myself down and retreating. Afterward, even though I knew that I'd never work for him and that I was the Elle Woods to his

WORK, BITCH

73

Warner Huntington III, I was disappointed in myself for making myself smaller for someone else. Luckily, I quickly realized that if I was going to succeed, I'd need to work with men who weren't threatened by the real me.

And while we're here, let's not forget the apologies that we make for our success and power, too. Men are encouraged, if not expected, to seize their power. To own it. To walk into a room and command it, knowing their worth. Bragging about their accomplishments and waving around their conquests. It's called Big Dick Energy for a reason. Women, on the other hand, aren't raised to do that. So we need to catch up on a steep learning curve. We may have been taught that boys don't like "girls like that," but do you really want to catch a man who can't handle a little Pussy Power? (I said it, and I'll say it again, all over chapter 5.) There might be a lot of things you're expected to do at work as part of your job, but making other people more comfortable is not one of them.

Now, there will obviously be times when you are truly sorry for something and an apology is due. In these cases, yes, owning up and genuinely apologizing is the classy thing to do. And it's all the more reason to stop throwing away all those other half-assed sorries—so people can start taking you more seriously when you say, and mean, the real thing.

<u>GET BITCHY</u>

Quitting the sorry habit starts with actually realizing how much you say it. Pay attention to how many times a day you say the word "sorry." Literally keep track on a sheet of paper, on the Notes app in your phone, or wherever you can keep a solid count. Do that for at least a week, or possibly a few weeks . . . however long it takes for you to start to see a pattern emerge. Can you identify in what settings or situations you tend to apologize unnecessarily? That's the first step to changing a habit.

Maybe you say "sorry" as the opener to most of your emails and texts since you feel like you're perpetually behind. "I'm so sorry I didn't get back to you," or "I'm sorry, I just saw this message, blah, blah, blah." This is actually a pretty easy fix: Just delete the opener and go right into the intended body of the message. Or sub in a personal note if the situation calls for it, like "It was great seeing you last week, hope you enjoyed your time off." Beyond that, chances are that (1) no one noticed that that email or text was missing and (2) no one cared if they did. And they definitely don't need a long, drawn-out explanation in place of a sorry. Get to the point.

For most of you, meetings with your coworkers are where you're going to rack up the most s-word infractions. Maybe it's just a tic that you can eventually cut out now that you're aware of it. But maybe it's something deeper—a result of feeling inadequate at work, or like you're going to risk stepping on toes if you assert yourself or your ideas. Explore that. Pay attention to how other people at the office communicate with each other. Do you see the men doing the same thing at meetings? Or your boss, male or female? My guess is no. Then do an experiment: Challenge yourself to speak up without apology—in your language or in your tone. How are your ideas received? How do you feel afterward? My money's on really fucking good.

Or, if you're in a situation where you feel like you really do have to change who you are or the way you speak to suit someone else, and that by being authentic you would risk losing your job, think long and hard about what that means for you. Think through what the worst-case scenario would be if you started to make small shifts in your behavior, no longer accommodating this toxic person or situation. Would it really be that bad, particularly if it meant that you'd no longer be cramming yourself into an unreasonably small box? We'll talk more about when it's time to walk away from a situation, but for now, meditate on that.

FAKE IT

There are those moments in your life when you have to make a choice between real and fake. Relationships? Real. Bags? Real. Money? Real AF. Face? Dealer's choice. But work? That's when you can make fake work for you. As I mentioned earlier, it's one of the best pieces of advice I ever got from my dad: "Fake it 'til you make it." I put this baby to the test when I was first trying to get a job and had zero experience—I faked having bartending experience (What, like it's hard?) and *may* have fudged my resume. (Who are we kidding, that thing was a greater work of fiction than *Moby* fucking *Dick*.) I leaned on it very time I went into an audition, hoping my cool confidence could convince a director to take a chance on an inexperienced actress. And I've reached for it again and again throughout my professional life in order to get where I wanted to go—even if I had no idea what I was doing.

When I was a baby real estate agent, I had a *lot* to learn. But I didn't think acting helpless and confused was a cute look, so I took a page from my dad's playbook. It made sense to me—I'd been acting since I was a little girl, pretending and trying on characters. I loved making movies with my video camera, directing my dolls, doing photo shoots, and generally being creative, and while I didn't know at the time what it was all adding up to, I knew that it had the power to make people feel a certain way, and I loved that. Since then, I have always had fun with pretending, and what I realized is that after a while, my brain wouldn't really know the difference. The result would be a genuine embodiment of whatever character I was trying on, which is a clutch skill to have if you're trying to make it as an actress—and, as it turns out, can also be helpful when you're trying to play the part of Boss Bitch.

In real estate, that meant that I first had to dress the part (or at least what I thought was the right costume at the time). Then, I made my reel for the role of killer real estate agent. The way I saw it, I could either let everyone know how inexperienced I was, or just not. It wouldn't hurt anyone to fudge the truth, and I always got people where they needed to go—but maybe in a more roundabout way. If a client asked me a question and I didn't know the answer, I'd say with complete authority: "That is a great question. I will find that out and get back to you right away." Or at open houses, when people were always drilling me with all kinds of questions, I'd give them my best guess and follow up later if I got it wrong. For example, if they asked me what year the house was built and I didn't really know, I'd give them an educated guess (unbeknownst to them), look it up later, then shoot them a text: "It was great seeing you today at my open house! I just wanted to follow up and let you know that the house was actually built in 2002, not 1996. Please let me know if you have any other questions!" First of all, it was kind of a genius hack, if you think of it—giving myself a reason to follow up with potential buyers. And second, even the most experienced real estate agent doesn't know everything. I didn't need to make them feel awkward or undercut my credibility by apologizing (lethal mistake #1) or explaining that I'm new and don't know anything (lethal mistake #2). I wanted to be taken seriously, so I acted seriously.

GET BITCHY

The best way to fake it is to find someone you admire and do your best impression until you become the real thing. It can be someone you see at the gym, at the office, on social media, in the tabloids, or on TV (moi?). Get all Marvel with that shit. Think the Black Widow would tweak over not knowing how to load paper into the fucking copy machine? Then examine what makes that person tick. Is it the way they walk? Talk? Dress? Move their body? Deal with conflict? Who is this person, their motivation? What do they sound like, look like? Then take those same qualities and adapt them to your own life. This souped-up version of you is now your Boss Bitch alter ego. She doesn't have to come out all the time, but she's who you call upon when you want to get shit done.

Paris Hilton is a prime example. She built an entire career around a character that she's really not but knows people love and has a lot of fun doing it. Look at her cooking show, where she acts like she's really stupid and can't scramble fucking eggs—this bitch has a billion-dollar perfume line and thirty-two companies. You really think she's that dumb? Of course not! She's really smart, but she plays into this character because it gives her an edge that's helped her succeed.

For me, my alter ego is someone I invented. Her name is Svetlana, and she's even more of a no-bullshit assassin than I am. She's who I channel when I go to work and need to *slay*. She loves rich men, richer women, Italian sports cars, and stilettos, and she definitely has a way with a whip.

It's OK if at first you don't feel like this person on the inside. That's actually the point of the exercise. The more you try to emulate this person, the more their qualities will soak into your brain, until it feels more natural to call upon those superpowers any time you need them.

ASK THE DAMN QUESTIONS

Another common trap that women fall into at work or in business is the fear of looking stupid or incompetent, and so they don't ask for help or dig deeper to get to the bottom of a situation. When I took the real estate licensing exam, it included questions like "Who passed the lead law in 1978?" And "How far do sex predators have to stay from a neighborhood community?" Not exactly applicable to the day-to-day of working in real estate. I did what I needed to do to memorize the answers for the test, but then when I started having actual real estate transactions cross my desk, I had no idea what I was doing. There was a seemingly endless amount of paperwork, and none of the rando answers I'd learned for my test came close to helping. At first I was too afraid to ask because I hated the feeling of being the new girl, and I was self-conscious about what people would think of me (how things have changed!). But I literally couldn't do my job until I worked up the courage to do it. I finally asked some of my colleagues about it, but no one seemed willing or able to help. They'd just shrug and go back to what they were doing. It was kind of weird. Then I asked my boss, Jason, and he said, "Well, don't worry about it; that's what Angelina and Eric are for," referring to the office associates who are in charge of the paperwork. "Leave it for them to handle."

I told Jason that I wanted to do it myself, if only to understand how the entire process works. I wanted to see firsthand all the different levels of a real estate deal.

"But I pay these people a salary to do that stuff," Jason said, clearly starting to lose patience with me. "You don't have to do this yourself."

He wasn't going to get it, so I pivoted and went to my coworker Nicole and told her that on my latest deal I wanted to do every step of the sale myself. She was incredibly helpful and taught me how to do each and every piece. I asked for help, and, as a result, I came away with a much more detailed understanding of the sale process than a lot of my competitors—er—coworkers. I didn't love having to admit that I didn't know something, and I definitely didn't love being talked to like I didn't have the ability to understand, but, in the end, I came out on top.

Sometimes you just have to take your ego out of the equation. If we don't ask for help or don't ask questions so we can learn how to do a better job at whatever it is we do, then we're only holding ourselves back. Do you ever find yourself Googling excessively before you'd dare ask a colleague how to do something at work? Do you feel like people will think you're dumb if you ask? Well, consider this: If a man were asking another man a question at work, the exchange would probably sound like this:

"Yo brah, show me how to use this thing."

"Yeah, bro, I'll show you; no problem, bro."

Ass slaps all around aaaand scene.

You don't have to make a big deal out of it, and you *definitely* don't have to apologize; you just need to have the balls to say,

"Hey, you know what? I need you to teach me how to do this so I can do it myself."

This is about much more than just a confidence issue. Because when you ask for help, you're also learning. Which means you're getting better at your job. Which means you're getting that much closer to being not just a Boss Bitch but being *The Boss*. (And even the boss needs to learn new things from time to time, too!) People are going to have opinions about you and judge you regardless—why not further your career in the process? And I promise, the more you do speak up and ask for what you need at work, the less uncomfortable you'll be doing it.

Another angle of the same issue is being afraid to raise questions in a situation where you need to advocate for yourself, especially when navigating a business deal. I learned that the hard way when I was working as an actress. I had a manager who discovered me (yeah, I know, it's so annoying and cheesy when people are like "I was discovered in a mall!"; but I really did get discovered!); he reached out after I did my first movie, *Shark Night 3D*. His name is Rob and his specialty was bringing in new talent and developing their career. From the very beginning we had an amazing relationship. He'd push me when I was doubting myself, telling me things like "Shut the fuck up and do it!" or "Don't forget who you are. C'mon!" And we'd bicker like an old married couple, like "Fuck you!" "Fuck you!" "Talk tomorrow; love you, bye!" He was like the Godfather meets Dance Moms. And I loved it. He was a powerful motivator and he recognized my value. We worked together for years, and he even met my family. During that time he got me so many great opportunities, to the point where he really put me on the map and people knew who I was. Eventually, I was approached by a huge agency—we're talking top five—and they wanted to represent me. They told me that they really wanted to work with me, took me out to fancy dinners, and gave me the whole schmooze and booze. I was so dazzled by everything they were promising that I decided to sign with them and let Rob go.

Well, I ended up sitting on their roster forever because I was just one of tons of other girls just like me who were represented by the agency. Until I finally got one job—and it was huge. It was such a big role and opportunity that I never stopped to ask any questions about it. I just flew out to Miami and shot my scenes with these huge celebrities. Then they wanted me to do a scene I wasn't really that comfortable with and didn't realize I had to do it because I'd never even thought to have asked, but I went ahead and did it because I was too afraid to say no. And after all that, my part got cut down . . . to that one scene. I called my agent and was like "What the fuck is this?" and his only response was "You got paid, what's your problem? That's business." I was heartbroken. Just totally shattered. Not only had I gone against my gut and turned my back on someone who genuinely cared about me (another big lesson in business—your intuition is everything!), but I never once stopped to ask some really important questions that would have prevented me from getting into this mess in the first place. I should have been asking my new agents what they had in mind for my career, or what kinds of roles they saw me in, or whether they'd let me do a two-week trial. But I'd committed a double-whammy business sin: I was too afraid to ask, and I hadn't done my homework.

What you need to realize is that asking questions doesn't make people think that you don't know your shit. It's the opposite: Drilling people with relevant questions shows them that you know your stuff and that you care enough to get the answers. And what's even more important is that now you have all the information you need to make an educated decision that protects your best interest. The most valuable asset you have is your intuition, and if you're not getting all your facts, you're not going to be able to fully assess a situation and weigh in with what your gut is telling you.

GO THE EXTRA MILE

When I was the new girl at the Oppenheim Group and just starting out in my real estate career, I was always looking for ways to set myself apart. I mean, struggling-actress-turned-real-estate-agent isn't exactly the most novel storyline here in LA. I quickly figured out that what I lacked in experience I could make up for in hustle with a splash of flair. Because while I may have had a lot to learn, no one works harder than me.

The first order of business was practice, practice, practice. Any time someone needed to babysit an open house, I'd volunteer. Any grunt work in the office? I'd gladly take it on. I was like that annoying summer intern hopped up on cheap coffee and dreams of greatness, except instead of running around like some clueless little puppy dog, I was on a mission. Oh, and I don't do coffee runs. I didn't think of it as paying my dues or like it was doing bitch work. Instead, I looked at the challenges of my new career through the lens of opportunity.

I also brought a healthy dose of optimism. I truly believed that my next client was just around the corner. If I so much as made eye contact with a new person in my first few weeks on the job, they got one of my business cards. And these business cards didn't come cheap. The company had them specially made with a personalized metal mold and thick paper embossed with our name and number. I didn't really have the money for them at the time, but I sucked it up and charged them to my credit card because I knew they'd legitimize me, at least in my own mind. And as we know by now, when something takes root in your brain, it's only a matter of time before it becomes real on the outside.

As soon as my cards arrived, I got to work meeting people. Whether it was at a yoga class or a happy hour, I'd meet someone, we'd chat, and then I'd say, "Here, let me give you my card." Handing over this tailored, thoughtful extension of me not only made me feel legitimate and luxe, it was also the first important step toward getting my name out there and meeting people who would ultimately become clients.

The next step for me was to take on open houses and own them as my personal projects. This wasn't hard to do because no one at the brokerage really wanted to do them. Open houses were held every Sunday and Tuesday, and it's a three- or four-hour deal each time. You don't get paid to do it, and there's no guarantee that anyone coming to see the house will make an offer to buy it. But I hoarded them. I took a pile of Jason's listings and offered to sit at each and every open house.

This was my best chance to practice in my new line of work. When people walked into one of these properties, they didn't know it was Jason's listing. It didn't matter. I was the person sitting there, so I got to answer their questions and rehearse my agent skills.

"Hi, welcome to such-and-such address, let me tell you all about the home. It's four thousand square feet, five bedrooms, four bathrooms. I'll show you around." To me, this felt like acting, or even like being a kid and playing again—it was fun for me. And by doing that over and over, I felt more confident in my skills as an agent. I'm so grateful for all those hours spent at open houses because they accelerated how quickly I advanced in my career and helped me to get to a place of true confidence faster. Once I started getting my own listings, I had all this experience behind me that I wouldn't have had if I had never volunteered for all that work that no one else wanted to do.

At the same time, calls started trickling in from people who had my fancy business card in their wallets, even months later. I'd get a voicemail like "Hi, we met back in the winter at that dance class and I thought of you because I'm getting ready to sell my house." All those early-stage bursts of effort began to pay off, and it was time to take things to the next level.

When I started doing open houses for my own listings, I wanted to make them special. So, at one of the very first, I brought cupcakes for people who came in to tour the property. Jason stopped by and looked confused.

"Why do you have cupcakes?" he asked me.

"Oh, it's just something I thought people would like," I said.

"Well, you don't have to do that," he told me.

"I know I don't *have* to," I replied. "But I *want* to."

I get where he was coming from—most agents would just show up with flyers, *maybe* some bottles of water. But to me, those little touches mattered. It personalized my open houses, and I truly believed that people would remember them. I'd bake cookies and light candles; I also read that in Chinese culture, it's good luck to have fruit in the kitchen, so I would put out bowls of oranges or lemons. I wanted to create an ambience that would help people feel like they were already home.

There was no way to quantify whether it worked—people don't put down an offer on a home and tell you, "You know, it was those amazing scented candles that really sealed the deal."

But subconsciously, I'm willing to bet that the extra effort stood out to people.

Going the extra mile also meant thinking outside the box on some occasions. One of my first clients was a woman who came through one of my open houses. She was this high-profile Boss Bitch who told me that this particular listing wasn't right for her, but she explained what she was looking for instead.

"Do you have an agent?" I asked her.

She didn't. I told her I'd love to help her find a home.

I was so excited to finally have a client of my own. I did so much work for her, took her on nearly a dozen private showings, and I looked at new listings in the MLS real estate database for her daily. We even started to become friendly, and she invited me to a party at her house. Then one day, I got a text from her about a property that I definitely hadn't taken her to see.

"Thanks so much for showing me that house. I'd love to put an offer on it," she wrote.

The text wasn't intended for me. She was working with another real estate agent.

That was a heavy blow. Truly; it felt like I'd just caught my signifcant other cheating. The audacity! I thought that she and I had formed a relationship, and I had no idea that she was working with someone else behind my back. I eventually found out that the other agent had shown her an off-market property and that's the one she offered on. So, while it definitely stung, personally and professionally, it was an important lesson for me to learn. I had to think outside the box in this business, and know that I had plenty of competition, some of which I couldn't even see.

In every job, you can do things by the book, or you can be prepared to go off script. After my high-profile client bought a house through another agent, I knew I had to get more creative.

I started talking to developers in order to get the inside track on up-and-coming properties before they even hit the market. I set up lunches and meetings with my rich friends to get a sense of what sort of properties were out there off the market and outside of the MLS. I could have taken this blow as a major setback and written it off as "Better luck next time." Instead, I decided to go out and make my own goddamn luck. And you better bet that it paid off.

Anyone, in any type of career, can go the extra mile and put in a little more work up front. At a minimum, you'll learn more, and more quickly. But beyond that, the possibilities are endless, especially if you're thinking of how to apply your own personal spin. Those touches are what bring your brand to what you do, and even though you might be selling the same cars as the chick one lot over, or offer the same accounting services as any other CPA in town, no one can do what you do the way that you do it. Going the extra mile in the spirit of your personal Boss Bitch style is a surefire way to amp up the value of your stock.

GET BITCHY

I want you to revisit the Five Boss Bitch languages, specifically the one that you matched with on the quiz in chapter 2. Now think about the values and attributes that are unique to your archetype and how you can hook them up with your regular business offerings to make yourself stand out. For example, if you're an Executive Boss Bitch, your extra mile might be offering a no-bullshit, always-punctual approach to your work among competitors who maybe take a beat too long to answer their texts and emails or follow up on business requests. Creative Boss

Bitches could think about adding a splash of color or graphic interest where other boring bitches are only dreaming in black and white. Matriarch Boss Bitches can add the special touch of making sure everyone feels taken care of, offering a signature drink or snack, taking a more personable approach instead of a slicker sell.

Now think of how you personally can take that up a notch. For me, that was the cupcakes at the open houses and the business cards printed on stock so nice it was yummy. Could you design a newsletter that goes out to clients or potential clients? Have a stack of tailor-made business cards with your own personal logo? It doesn't necessarily have to be expensive, but I guarantee if you dig deep for that extra flourish, it'll pay off.

BE A QUITTER

I know it's a hot take, but I truly believe that in order to fully step into your power at work, you have to get comfortable with the idea of quitting if it really came down to it. Because walking away from something when it's no longer serving you is called having boundaries. And let me tell you, that's my second-favorite B word. Boundaries mean you know exactly what you are and are not willing to do, and no one can trifle with that. Having boundaries is the same as having a code, a personal belief system. And that shit is powerful. Far too many women falsely equate quitting with failure, and that is simply not a belief that's going to serve you well in business. You will most likely have jobs that won't be the right fit for you, bosses who don't treat you well, or coworkers you don't vibe with. You have a choice: You can stay and talk yourself into being happy, or you can find something better—which you almost certainly will. So forget the old, played-out "don't be a quitter" trope, and be open to the idea of getting the fuck out if need be.

From a very young age I was always able to say No. I knew my mind and wasn't afraid to speak it. It's such a simple two-letter word, but no is one of the hardest things that you can say to people. But I just intuited that I needed to say No and walk away from situations that I knew I didn't want to be in. And as a result, I learned early on the power of taking myself out of situations that didn't feel right, organic, or authentic for me. For example, I quit or got fired from nearly every job I had as a teenager because I was always standing up for myself. When I was sixteen and working at Sonic, they introduced a rule that it would be mandatory for all employees to deliver food on roller skates. I said, "That's fucking dangerous! I don't want to break an ankle. I'm not a roller skater. I can't do that." But my boss told me that it was corporate policy and that I had to do it unless I had a doctor's note. I went home and forged a pretty good one, which lasted me a while. But ultimately they found out that I didn't have a legitimate medical excuse, and because I still refused to wear the skates, they let me go.

I had a similar exit from Taco Bell when I was fifteen. I've always loved getting my nails done, and while I was working at the fast-food chain, I spent $40 on a new set of acrylic nails—a lot of money to me back then. My nails had never been an issue, but one day my boss told me that they were a food hazard because one could inadvertently come off into the food. If I wanted to keep my job, I'd have to have my acrylics removed before coming back. So I quit.

Now, I know this might sound a little silly at face value. You quit your job over roller skates and a set of nails? But my job exits never came from a place of wanting to be rebellious; it came from not wanting to sell myself short for a job. For whatever reason, I was able to see that there would always be other options, that I should find a job that fit me and my needs and desires, not the other way around. I brought that attitude with me into my acting career, and then eventually into real estate.

When I first started acting, it was so much fun and really fulfilling. From the time I acted in my middle school plays, I always had a passion for performing, so doing it as my actual job seemed too good to be true. When I still lived in Dallas, I got cast in a movie called *Shark Night 3D*, which is when I officially caught the bug. I'd been modeling, but doing that movie changed everything. I moved to LA and started auditioning. During those years, I felt this deep excitement about the work; every audition was an adventure and I got a lot of parts.

But after a while, the charm wore off and work was less available. I started to get typecast as the stereotypical dumb blonde. Auditions became fraught with the pressure of: If I don't get this job, what am I doing to do? My heart wasn't in it anymore, and I began to resent the work because I primarily needed it for the money. More than anything else, I felt that familiar constraint on my freedom—the part of my life that I value most. I wasn't in control of whether or not I would get cast. A casting director could be having a bad day, or could have a better relationship with another actress, or personal connections, like the daughter of a friend of their mom (it happens!).

No matter how good I was, at the end of the day, did I really want to put my fate and future into the hands of a washed-up actress with a frizzy Fantastic Sams blowout and six rescue cats? As the great poet Ariana Grande would say, "Thank you, next." I believe that as soon as you start resenting the thing you once loved, it's time to move on. That carefree, nonchalant attitude I used to have was gone, and the fire died. My intuition told me it was time to make a change, and I knew that I didn't want to end up as one of those forty-year-old former soap-opera actresses still trying to catch her big break.

So I pivoted. When I knew I was ready for a career move but didn't yet know what it would be, an ex-boyfriend introduced me to his friend, Jason Oppenheim. (And trust me, it was the only good thing that came out of that relationship.) Even I knew that he was a big name in the real estate business in Los Angeles. Still, I had my doubts at first. "Trust me," my friend said. "Real estate is all about people and you're really good with people. You'll do great." I had lunch with Jason, we got along well, and my interest in the business was piqued. Jason said, "Come back when you get your real estate license."

Just the idea of taking the real estate licensing exam was pretty daunting. School just wasn't my thing, especially thanks to my ADD. But I knew I had to buckle down and get over this hurdle if I wanted to try out working in real estate. So I got a prescription for Adderall and decided that if I was going to do this, I was going to need to pass the test as quickly as I could. The longer I drew it out, the longer it would be until I could make money or live life on my own terms.

To be completely honest, I didn't have a particular affinity for real estate. Sure, I love a gorgeous house as much as the next flossy bitch—I mean, they're like models who don't talk back during fittings. But what I truly love is connecting with people and helping them, in this case, finding exactly what they want in a home. But the appeal for me went beyond the work itself. Being a real estate agent meant that I could go out and attract my own clients, choose who I wanted to work with, and be in control of how much work I did and when. And while Jason and his brother Brett owned the Oppenheim group and I was technically one of their employees, I still essentially worked for myself as an independent contractor living the 1099 life. In other words, real estate meant I could maintain my freedom, which is what I value the most in this world.

Back to that exam. I studied the hell out of that test for three weeks. I sat down every night with flash cards that I made myself, navigating a crash course in real estate that I invented using apps that I'd downloaded and *Real Estate for Dummies*. I'd order Pizza Hut for dinner and study. Nothing else. It was actually the first time I took a test really, really seriously because I finally cared about the subject matter. And after all that work, I passed. I eventually found out that that was basically unheard of—I was told that most people take three to six months to get their license, and many don't pass the first time they take the test. But I was driven, and suddenly I had a whole new career. (Thanks, Teva Pharmaceuticals!)

After years of learning the hard way that when I don't see the point in trying hard at something, I have zero motivation to do it (Reason 572 high school didn't work out so well for me). I also learned to realize I don't get motivated from being bossed around, or told what to do (only in the bedroom, please and thank you). It wasn't until I got out into the world and found my passion that I realized I wasn't lazy after all! Once I put my mind to something I really want to do, I could really work it.

It's a pretty unmistakable feeling when that fire inside your belly goes out. It's up to you to pay attention to it. Don't ignore the resentment that can start creeping into your professional life. Listen to that little voice in your head when it tells you that something isn't right or that you're not happy. If you're the type of person who's inclined to make a list of pros and cons before making a career move, do that. Or if you're more into how things feel, try really staying in the moment the next time your gut starts raising an alarm. In the end, it comes down to trusting yourself. The more you practice tuning into your intuition, the easier trusting it will be.

After years of perfecting this skill of tuning into what I need and want, I've gotten really good at taking inventory of my life, adding more of what's working, and cutting out what's not. That's why, when real estate stopped being as fun as it was when I first started, it didn't scare me when I decided to walk away. Instead, it excited me because I couldn't wait to see what was next. In my case, I wanted even more freedom to be myself and express my creative side. That's why I'm working on building my empire, because I've always loved things like beauty, fashion, and inspiration, and now I can call all the shots.

<u>LIGHTEN UP</u>

I know this may come as a shock to you, but I don't give a shit what people think about me—including in business. I put this cardinal rule in the same category as not apologizing and not being afraid to ask for help: You have to put aside what people think of you in order to reach your full Boss Bitch potential. When I'm working, I'm the consummate professional. I'm punctual, I respect people's time, and I hustle my ass off in order to hold up my end of the working relationship. But at the end of the day, you can't take yourself too seriously because when you do, then you're basically admitting that you're worried about what other people will think about you. If, however, you come across like you don't give a fuck, then—maybe ironically—people will love you more for it because it makes you more relatable and it projects the kind of confidence that people like to be around.

I mean, just look at the show. Do you think I got where I did by being afraid of showing people who I really am or taking myself so seriously that I was closed off? Instead, I made myself vulnerable. I didn't get caught up with being perfect every single second like some of the other girls who care waaaaay too much about what people will think about them if they get into an argument on-camera (what I like to call "the producer's special") or play ball with a little manufactured drama. I loved filming scenes with Amanza because we could be ridiculous and over-the-top and totally get into it, then completely laugh it off once the cameras were done rolling. Or the episode where I can't get into my listing. Do you really think I wouldn't be able to get into my own listing? Of course I have the fucking keys. That was totally fabricated for television. There's a film crew of seventy people filming inside who have had a permit from the city of West Hollywood to shoot at that location for at least a week prior—do you think that no one has access to the front door? I could have made a fuss about how it would make me look unprofessional, but I went with it because I thought it was funny and I'm a good sport. So I was just like "Oh yeah, sorry; guess we can't get in . . . ooops!" And then Heather and I had to get into this fake fight—which I thought we did a really good job of doing. At the end of the day, I know how hard I work in real life; I know that I'm fucking amazing at what I do. And I'm also pretty confident that no one watching the show is gonna go, "She's such a shitty real estate agent." And even if they did, I know that that's not true; and that's all that matters.

Making great television aside, this rule applies just as easily to real life. If I ever make a mistake or look like an ass at work, I just laugh it off. Shit happens. It's way too exhausting to pretend to be perfect—because let's be honest, we all know it's impossible. Who are you trying to fool? Focus that energy instead on slaying your to-do list and making money moves—those actions speak a lot louder than anyone's words can.

CHAPTER 5

MIND YOUR VAGINA

I want to take a moment to talk about relationships. But this isn't *Cosmo* Find Your True Love. This is all about owning one of the most powerful assets that all women (and in spirit, some men, too—I see you, boos) have: the Power of the Pussy. Don't go clutching your pearls on me now; this is serious shit if you're really set on unleashing your full potential as a Boss Bitch.

What put Pussy Power into perspective for me was after I gave birth to Christian. I thought if I can grow, sustain, and birth a baby—or have one Edward Scissorhanded out of me—then I can do fucking anything. I don't mean that we all need to go out and have babies in order to tap into it, but what I do mean is that Pussy Power is primal. It comes with the complete set of living as a woman, and it's the most powerful, sacred thing of all humankind. Don't just take it from me, fucking evolution says so.

The fact is—and I know you all know this—we have a unique allure that, when harnessed and executed correctly, makes a man, and even some women, defenseless. I'm not saying that to be manipulative—though, yeah, it kind of is in the best possible way. I'll never forget when I first learned about the Power of the P: I'd basically been living under a rock when it came to sex until I was fifteen years old. Because of my parents' plan to hide me away from the world, and that whole Catholicism thing, they never taught me anything having to do with my body, and especially not doing the dirty. Add to the fact that I lived in Texas, where sex ed is essentially nonexistent, and I was clueless. One day, I was out walking dogs in the neighborhood with a girl who lived nearby. She told me that she kissed a guy, and no joke, my response was "Oh my gosh! Aren't you afraid you're going to get pregnant?!" If she wasn't so shocked, she would have laughed in my face. Instead, I think she felt bad for me instead, and she did her best to explain the birds and the bees then and there. Suffice it to say, Mind. Blown.

After that, though, I started dating a guy who was a little older and started to learn what was what when it came to hooking up. I was like, *OK, I get it now.* And there was no turning back. I always felt like I was sexy, even before I knew what sex was, so it was just one more way for me to express my confidence and have fun while doing it. After my bad-boy boyfriend, I decided to have a good time with sex, ho-ing it up and calling the shots with who, where, what, and when. I had totally stepped into my power and saw no reason it wasn't something to be harnessed and used as a tool. I loved toying with guys and breaking their hearts, dating a few boys at the same time, and having two guys ask me to prom. If we're being honest, I got a sick pleasure out of making guys do what I wanted. I'd break up with them, and they'd be all puppy dog–eyed and whimpering about it. Want to know why? Because I'd gotten in touch with a deep, vibrational part of myself that went way beyond the physical. I wasn't just another beautiful woman. I was smart, funny, witty. I had substance *and* style. And most importantly, I had value. I realized that I was not replaceable. People would see me making my man work for things in my relationships (sex, the upper hand, the last word—aka power) and be like "They're going to go out and find another girl." Maybe, but they wouldn't find another me. Because I have magic. We all have magic. We all have this natural Aphrodite inside ourselves.

I'm not saying that we need to go out and whip our partners into submission (unless they're into that, in which case, don't forget the leather, bitch). That wouldn't be very satisfying either. What I am saying, though, is that when you harness your Pussy Power and come at a relationship from a place of your values, standards, and self-worth, then you're setting the stage for a real relationship. One that's built on the sturdiest foundation meant for the long-haul and not just one that will crumble after the first ho with a tight ass walks by.

To help you pussy up, I've put together my most important relationship rules that I've discovered through my years of dating in the notoriously tricky LA singles scene, and then eventually finding Mr. Christine Quinn (or Christian, as he keeps insisting on being called). Follow these and you'll be on the right path to finding the perfect partner for you—or keeping the partner you have—and creating a relationship based on truth, respect, real love, and the kind of spark that you can't fake.

RULE #1 NEVER SETTLE . . . AND "SOUL MATES" ARE BULLSHIT

Let me tell you about the first man I ever got serious with, Mr. Going Nowhere. Back when I was eighteen and working as a waitress at a cocktail bar Erika Jayne–style, I met one of the first men that I got serious about. At the time, I was doing my best impression of the shit-talking, no-fucks-given bartenders working there. I was in awe of how they rarely followed the rules, always gave shit to their bosses, and came in a cool twenty minutes late for shift meetings, reeking of cigarettes and independence. To me, that was fucking cool. (Did I mention that I was eighteen?)

Then one night I met this guy. He was cute, in a preppy Goldman Sachs way, but I didn't take him seriously at first. I just chalked him up as That Guy Who Goes to Bars to Meet Girls—who I had made a rule of never dating. But then I learned that he was there to celebrate a friend's birthday that night, so I gave him a pass. When I finished my shift, he asked me out. We went to the Waffle House, which was the only restaurant still open late-night. I proceeded to order the All-Star (the most expensive thing on the menu at a whopping $7.99). We got to talking, and he immediately struck me as a kind soul and someone who wasn't quick to pass judgment on others. Mr. Going Nowhere was a classic Texas guy, a gentleman, a breath of fresh air, and he seemed to be into my reckless, potty-mouthed attitude laced with my lethal "bless your heart" Southern smile. Before long, he was my rock. He was loyal to me, supportive of my pursuit of an acting career and pretty much anything else I told him that I wanted to do with my life.

A couple of years later, when I was twenty, we took a ski trip to Tahoe with our families. The idea of flying down a mountain on two slices of polished wood scared the shit out of me, and the snow and cold were definitely not my scene, but I tried to put on a happy face for my man. Then one day, we were out taking a walk when I noticed he was acting all nervous and flustered. Then he whipped something out of his pocket.

"Will you marry me?" he asked, presenting me with . . . an empty box.

I stared at the box and then back at my boyfriend.

"Oh, shit!" he said, as we both realized the ring had gone flying into the snow.

"Wait, is this real?" I asked as he began digging through the powder like an eager golden retriever.

"There was a ring in the box!" he insisted. I joined him in the hunt, and we eventually found the ring. I accepted his proposal . . . and the weird, unsettled feeling that came with it. Getting engaged that young was the norm in Dallas, just like graduating high school and going to college. It was simply the next box to check. But you know by now how I feel about checking boxes.

On paper, I had everything with Mr. GN. But I knew that if I stayed with him, I'd end up barefoot and pregnant within a few years. Mr. GN was status quo. And there's nothing wrong with the status quo—or being barefoot and pregnant, for that matter, if it's what you want. But I wanted more than just a reliable, supportive man. If I wanted reliable and supportive, I'd buy another fucking bra. I wanted a fabulous, whirlwind life on top of it. I wanted a career as an actress in a big city; and I wanted to see the world, one fabulous adventure after the next. That just wasn't Mr. GN's style.

The night of my engagement at the ski lodge, I pulled my mom aside. "I can't do this," I told her, my stomach sinking at the thought of spending my life with my now-fiancé. "This is not what I want."

My mom wasn't entirely surprised. "But he's such a great guy," she said.

I pictured myself putting aside my dreams and settling down with Mr. GN in Texas with a baby and a mortgage by the time I was twenty-three.

Over the next couple of months, I started doing what I now realize was manifesting but had no idea at the time. It was just an instinct to really focus on the things I hope would come true. I wanted a glamorous life, so I started imagining myself living that way, looking the part, and proving to the world that I could make it, even without checking the standard boxes. In fact, I threw out the whole fucking checklist and made my own.

I pored over fashion magazines, just as I'd done when I was younger, and envisioned myself in the clothes and the shoes I saw on the pages. I'd go to the mall and try on pieces I couldn't afford, acting as if this was the life that I had, even if I didn't have it yet. I even bought a Louis Vuitton bag, just to be able to see it in my apartment before taking it back to the store (my first real lesson in manifesting, but more on that in chapter 7).

Things were comfortable with Mr. GN, but he had no interest in pursuing the lifestyle I wanted. We were just too different. And by that I mean a deal-breaker well beyond him not wanting to go for sushi or wear a dress shirt every once in a while. I mean differences that were at the depths of our souls, the things that motivated us and made us really, truly happy. So, I broke off our engagement. And with that, I also wrote my first rule for relationships: **Never settle for just being comfortable.** If one person can't offer you the things you want most in life, you should go out and find someone else who can.

So often when people feel that "click" with another person— that feeling that everything is just right, that they can really be themselves together—they often like to make the leap to thinking that they're soul mates and that they were "meant to be." Well, I don't believe in that. Truthfully, I think the concept of soul mates is total bullshit. I mean, it's just not logical—there are more than 7.6 billion people on this planet. You're telling me that if you meet someone and fall in love . . . that's it? You're just meant to be with this one person forever? Out of all the people on the planet? There are easily thousands of people who would want to be with you, and you could go on to fall in love with any number of them. If you ask me, the idea of "soul mates" is just another story that we've been sold, like a trashy romance novel. That's why I think that you need a higher bar when assessing whether you've found The One. Love is great, but it's not the only thing that makes a relationship work. Or, more importantly, work for you.

RULE #2: NEVER SACRIFICE WHAT YOU VALUE MOST

After Mr. Going Nowhere and I ended our engagement, my next relationship was with Mr. V, the handsome stranger who walked into my bar and said he wanted to buy me Valentino and Louboutins. We soon started dating—not because he took me shopping but because he was irresistibly magnetic. Mr. V was gorgeous, for starters: tanned skin, blue eyes, and slicked-back blonde hair. He was also interesting, smart, worldly, and sophisticated . . . exactly what I wanted to be when I got older. Despite our significant age gap (he was forty and I was twenty-one), we found ourselves on the same page about everything from politics and current events to just day-to-day life. I was convinced that with him I could finally have my ideal life of excitement, travel, and luxury.

Was he a sugar daddy? Yes. Was he someone with whom I had a real connection? Also yes. Pretty much overnight, I got everything that I'd wished for and manifested back when I went to the mall to try on outfits I thought I could never afford. That first shopping spree easily set Mr. V back $100,000.

A week later, he doubled down and bought me a brand-new Bentley. (In his name, of course.)

We moved in together in his swank Dallas mansion.

We traveled as often as we felt like it, hopping aboard his brand-new Gulfstream and staying in five-star hotels all over the globe.

It always came back to fashion for Mr. V—he was obsessed with clothes and shopping. He'd been married before, and he spent exorbitant amounts of money on his ex-wife and himself at Roberto Cavalli, earning himself VIP status at the Dallas boutique. I thought Cavalli was such a fancy, grown-up designer at the time, the same way I felt about Valentino. These were names I'd seen on the runway and in magazines, not labels I'd ever expected to see in my closet.

That was about to change.

One night, Mr. V pulled some of those VIP strings and closed down the Dallas boutique. He invited my sister and one of my best friends to join me for a private shopping experience. Roberto Cavalli himself flew his latest collection from Paris Fashion Week to Dallas. *Just for me.* It was a scene straight out of a movie, but more exclusive and more over-the-top. Sales associates were opening vintage bottles of Dom Perignon as I took in this insane amount of animal prints, feathers, chains, and leather. It was the first time I'd seen couture in person, and it was more exquisite than I could have imagined. I got fitted for the pieces I liked best and modeled them for my sister and my friend. I had a fashion geek-out moment, too, getting to examine the structure and craftsmanship of the dresses. A couture gown is truly a piece of art—and I had a store full of them to choose from.

But life with Mr. V wasn't all champagne and couture. Another suitable nickname for him might have been Mr. Old Fashioned, as he was a super-rich guy from Texas who just wanted a housewife. Nothing more. He wasn't excited by my acting aspirations. He wanted me home, and he wanted to do everything together. It was his world—I was just living in it.

I was literally surrounded by luxury, exactly as I'd manifested it. I got the fabulous, whirlwind life I wanted, but I didn't have a dollar to my name since he didn't give me a credit card, or any money of my own. If I felt like getting Starbucks, Mr. V. would say, "Great. I'll come with you." If I wanted to go shopping, he would take me. I found a way to live the lifestyle I'd desired, but I lost what I valued most: freedom. All of the material possessions in the world, even those imported from Paris, couldn't make up for that.

It would ultimately be that Bentley Mr. V bought me just a week into our relationship that would lead to our demise as a couple. He was always asking me not to eat McDonald's in the Bentley. (Don't act surprised, bitches. Anyone who says they're too fancy for McDonald's is a fucking liar.) I told Mr. V that I wasn't eating it in the car, even though I totally had been. I figured there was no harm in a little white lie since I always cleaned up really well after myself, and besides, what the fuck did he care?!

One day I was out in the Bentley with a friend, and on the way home, we grabbed dinner (Big Mac, no pickles, Dr Pepper,

French fries, honey mustard, and ketchup—forever and always). As usual, I was careful to clean up afterward. Short of bringing in an entire forensic team to investigate, there was no way Mr. V would know we'd eaten in the car.

But when I got home, he had a stern expression on his face. "I know you went to McDonald's," he said.

That's when I realized something strange was going on. Had he put a tracking device on the car? Tracked my phone? Somehow he always knew where I'd been. Mr. V bought me all these really nice things, and he expected certain things from me in return, like being the Barbie on his arm so he could parade me around like a trophy. And that was fine—I loved it. But my freedom? That was a non-negotiable. I knew I needed to end the relationship, even with all the perks. I never did call him out on the tracking device, though. I didn't have the confidence or the power. It was just another form of apologizing for myself back then—something I've since learned never again to do. He had no right to keep tabs on me like that, let alone sacrifice my privacy. That's something that no amount of money could buy. Ultimately, our breakup was pretty mutual. He knew that I wanted to be more than a housewife.

I didn't see that as a setback, though. Dating these two very different men showed me that I could, actually, have it all. But first, I needed to hold up my end of the deal. That's right, I couldn't just sit back and wait for some perfect guy to give me everything I wanted—I had to meet him part of the way. Just like we'll talk about in the manifesting chapter (my personal fave and the secret sauce to beating the final Boss Bitch level), it's one thing to sit around and wish for something great to happen; it's a whole other story to give your dreams a motor through your own targeted actions. In my case, I realized I would never find my Knight in Shining Armani if I didn't take steps to save myself. And that started with moving to Los Angeles to pursue my career.

I had only just begun thinking about how I would manage this, given that I hadn't been working since Mr. V made me quit, and there was no way I'd be able to finance the move myself. But Mr. V was so kind to me and offered to help. The deal was that I would stay in Texas for a little while longer, working and saving up as much money as I could, while he would hire a moving company and ship my car to California. He wanted me to succeed in the life I wanted, even if it wasn't with him.

The bottom line is that it's your job to make sure the person you end up with will fit into the whole picture of the life you want for yourself. This goes back to asking yourself what you value, just like you did in chapter 1. For me, it was luxury, adventure, and excitement without sacrificing my independence. Sure, I wanted to find someone who loved me for me, but I refused to believe that I'd have to sacrifice my values for the first guy who said "I love you." So I diversified my portfolio. I dated more and more men until I found someone who fit that exact mold: the one who would not only support me and my dreams but also help me make them happen—who wanted to take the world by storm, who had his own aspirations for success, and who also wasn't intimidated by a successful woman.

Yeah, sometimes I had setbacks, like one of my ex-boyfriends, Mr. Mafia. (Seriously; I'm pretty sure it's not just a cute nickname.) He was fabulous in every way—loved designer clothes, drove the flossiest cars, the works (it was some next-level *Succession* shit)—and he was really good to me, too. But eventually it became clear that he had a negative relationship with drugs. Things never got violent, but manically rolling up to Blick to buy 572 paintbrushes and acrylic paints and painting and playing chess until five A.M. was not exactly my scene, either. It was really hard, watching things decline at work, with his friends, and in life. I wanted nothing to do with it because I was already terrified of drugs, thanks to my prison stint, and I also decided that my happiness wasn't worth going along for this ride. The boy loved blow more than he'd ever love me, and I was worth more than that.

Little by little I rewrote that checklist and filled it with the qualities that I knew would help me live my best life. You have to do the exact same thing. Make a list of what you need a guy to have beyond just being a "good partner." Be picky. Be savage. This is the rest of your life! And at the end of the day, the guy you pick might not be your "soul mate," but they are damn lucky.

RULE #3: BE HONEST ABOUT WHAT YOU (EVENTUALLY) WANT

By the time I met my now-husband, Christian, I was twenty-nine and I'd been in a lot of relationships and on what felt like hundreds of dates. I was ready to settle down—or at least my version of it. By this point, I knew that the only way to stop dicking around was to be as up front as possible about my wants and needs. So on my very first date with Christian, we had The Talk about what we each wanted for the future. I knew it was ballsy, but I had zero interest in waiting around for six months while we ultimately came to the conclusion that this was going nowhere. I said to him, "Here's what I'm looking for in a relationship: I'm looking for something serious, and I eventually want to get married and have kids. If you don't want these things, then I'm not here to waste your time—and I definitely don't want you to waste mine." I made it clear that I didn't assume that was going to happen with him in particular—I mean, come on, it was our first date—but those were my goals, full stop, no take-backs.

I know what you're thinking: That's like a major violation of The Rules, or some other nonsensical bullshit that we've all had poured down our throats along with our lemon drop shots. But think about where being afraid to ask the hard questions has gotten you? How many relationships have wasted your valuable time because you didn't pussy up and be clear about what you wanted and needed? Or let me guess, waited around because you thought maybe you could eventually want what he wants? Gag. For me, I realized that I had spent way too much of my young adult life not wanting to let my wants and needs be known because I was worried I'd scare my boyfriends away. And you know where that got me? Absofuckinglutely nowhere. Instead, I realized that one of the most valuable things we have in the whole entire world is time—it's the only currency we have on this earth. So I wasn't about to waste that on some dude who wasn't on the same page as me. From the moment I came to terms with that, I would always ask straight-up on the first date: Do you want what I want? Did plenty of guys not call me back? Yeah. But were they the right people for me? No. It doesn't have to be a *60 Minutes* interview—you don't have to grill them—but you should gauge their interest and make sure you're speaking the same language when it comes to the direction that your relationship is heading.

Lucky for me—and a big fat duh considering we're happily married and have a beautiful baby together—Christian didn't even bat an eye at my forwardness. He confirmed that he was looking for the same things that I was, and he was true to his word.

I get that it can be a little nerve-racking, but after spending time with this book and stepping into your own power, you'll hopefully see that you *deserve* to know what kind of man or woman you're about to spend that hard-earned time on. If your potential partner wants what you want, and you're both honest about it right away, then you're in a good position to get the relationship off to a good start. And if they're too scared to have that conversation early on, what else is going to scare them off? It's better to know right away if the person you're dating can handle a woman speaking up about what she wants. This doesn't mean you need to get serious right away, of course. More on that in Rule #6.

RULE #4: NEVER EVER HAVE SEX ON THE FIRST DATE

On my first date with Christian, we went out for a steak dinner (Japanese Kobe for me, obvi), and I could immediately tell that he was different. In LA, you often get this entitled vibe from guys—they feel like they deserve to be out on a date with gorgeous women. You can imagine how quickly that gets old! With Christian, I could tell he was appreciative to be there at dinner, which alone was refreshing. But also, he was treating me like an actual person—and not just that, the intelligent goddess that I knew I was even though no one ever treated me like it. He was listening to everything that I said, which meant our banter was amazing. We laughed a lot, and I could tell he was nervous, too, which was really cute.

When dinner was over and the check was paid, we said goodnight . . . and that was it. The next dozen or so dates ended the same way. After a few weeks of dating, Christian wanted to take me to Aspen. I told him, "I'm not having sex with you yet, so you'd better have a separate bedroom for me. End of conversation." We didn't end up going on the trip; namely because I wasn't about to play into his not-so-hidden agenda.

I waited *three months* before sleeping with him. Not because I wasn't seriously hot for the guy—because I was—but because I knew how to use Pussy Power to my advantage. Remember when I told you beautiful girls in LA are basically a bulk commodity? Smart, successful, good-looking guys like Christian just have to walk out their front door to find some basic bitch to join them for dinner and an easy lay. Seriously, if you're quiet for a second on a Saturday night, it's like you can hear the panties dropping around town for the first guy in a Lambo that they meet. But not this girl. I work way too hard to be giving anything away for free. It didn't always work out in my favor, but that was the exact information I needed to know about the guy I was interested in. If he wasn't man enough to wait, then he definitely wasn't man enough for me. Christian, on the other hand, was hooked.

After we got married, he told me that I had driven him fucking crazy and that no one before me had ever held out like that. He was talking to multiple girls at the time, but the fact that I didn't just put out or even text him back right away whenever he would reach out (another great way to keep a guy thinking about you) drove him nutty. According to him, that's what made him fall so deeply for me and want nothing to do with those other girls. It wasn't just that he couldn't have me—though I do think that's a big part of it because men are really just a bunch of toddlers pumped up with testosterone—it was that I clearly valued myself enough to do things on my own schedule, when it felt right to me.

I'll never understand women who have sex with a guy they just met and then act all surprised when he doesn't call them back. I'm not saying that there's not a time and a place for a one-night stand (see Rule #5), and I'm definitely not that girl who is going to drive-by slut shame for wanting to get your rocks off. I've been there. But there's so much else that you have to offer a partner besides sex. So I'm saying that it's worthwhile to give them a chance to get to know those sides of you before things get physical. Here's a great example: I have a friend, let's call her Karen, who, bless her heart, is kind of a huge ho and she knows it. She was living with me for a little while, and she would go on dates with guys, then be like "I don't understand—I gave him a BJ in the car/gave him a BJ in the hot tub/fucked him in the bathroom, and now I haven't heard from him." It kept happening over and over and over again.

So I'm like, "Girl, of *course* they're not calling you back." And I explained to her why. She got it, but then she met the guy of her absolute dreams. She was terrified of messing it up because she really wanted a ring on that finger. So I said to her, "Here's what you have to do—." Then I proceeded to tell her exactly what I'm about to tell you. Because, by the way, I'm totally coming back as a therapist in the next life because I give THE BEST advice. So anyway, here's what you're going to do: You're not going to fuck him. End of story. You're not even going to kiss him at the end of the date. Wipe that look off your face—do you want that Mrs. degree or what? She did it, and it worked—more dates, things got a little more serious.

But then his birthday rolled around and she freaked again. I'm telling you, some girls think that the only thing they have that's worth anything is what's in their panties. I don't care how vajazzled that thing is, it's not the most valuable thing you have to offer. So I asked her, "What is your goal in this relationship?" To which she said, "I want to get married." OK, now we're talking. I said, "Do this and I guarantee you'll be engaged in a year: Write him a card and say, 'Don't open this until our one-year anniversary.'" She did it, and sure as shit, they got engaged and are now married.

It's a prime example of making decisions that are in line with your goals. Looking to have fun and not take the relationship seriously? Have all the sex you want. But if you want it to last, then maybe not right out of the gate. By doing that, you're giving your new man or woman time to get to know you and value the things about you that you're most proud of—your mind, your wit, your sense of humor. Yes, you can be super proud of your tits and ass, too—I know I am—but they're not the only things about me that make me special.

So, if you're out on a date and you think there's potential, think of me perched on your shoulder like your sexy fairy godmother, reminding you of the cardinal rule: No sex on night one! Minimum. If you want a guy to take you seriously in a relationship, you have to make them wait. Let them get to know you and appreciate you. Let them picture you naked and all the things they want to do to you. Let their imagination run wild. And then, let your freaky-deaky self do all the freaky-deaky things. Trust me, the buildup is worth it.

RULE #5: BUT ALSO, THERE'S NO SHAME IN ONE-NIGHT STANDS

I firmly believe that if you're interested in having a serious, long-lasting relationship with a man, then you absolutely cannot, under any circumstances, have sex on the first date. But that doesn't mean that you can't have sex with someone you've just met, so long as your intention is to keep things exclusively sexual, aka Status: Fuck Buddy. We are allowed to be sexual creatures and completely own that we like getting some quality action as much as the guys do; you just have to own that if you want to scratch that itch and you haven't built a solid emotional foundation with your partner, then things most likely aren't going to make it beyond Level O. Before I got married, there were many times where I didn't want anything more than one night with a guy. Instead of channeling that pent-up energy into going on dates, I looked to the original source of the one-night hookup: apps like Tinder and Tingle. Then I made sure that we were both on the same page, knowing that tonight was about having a good time and nothing more.

And don't make the mistake that so many women have made before you: Do not, under any circumstances, try to domesticate the fuck boy. There's a reason he answers your texts, and it's not because you're up on current events. Guys who are happy to regularly indulge in booty calls are most likely still wanting to keep things casual. They might tell you otherwise in order to keep that good stuff on tap, but those guys are nothing more than the all-too-common Fuck Boy and will ghost you faster than you can say "move in together."

RULE #6: DON'T RUSH IT

I didn't just hold off on getting naked with Christian; I didn't call or text him, either. I *always* let him call or text me. And when he did, I'd say something like "Oh, I can't meet up tonight, but I'll get back to you once I figure out my schedule." Part of the reason was that I was truly busy with work and filming the show. But I also knew that by being just a bit out of reach, I was letting him know that I wasn't going to be such an easy get. I required a little pursuit and persuasion. After we got married, Christian eventually told me that my approach had worked—it made him *want* to work for it. And not only that, it made him feel like if I wasn't running to answer his calls to go on dates, then I most likely wasn't doing it with other guys either. I don't know about you, but I'd always like people to think that getting into my club is more Soho House than Hard Rock Cafe. I have a life, and I'm not going to drop everything just for a guy. And I also wanted him to know that when I did make time for him, I was being really intentional about it. Nothing is more attractive to a man than a woman who has her own life, her own hobbies, and her own things going on.

Playing hard to get is a classic move that never goes out of style. If a man isn't driven enough to call, then he isn't the man for me. I need someone who is going to go the distance to get the woman he wants—and that's exactly what Christian did. I don't ever want to have to convince somebody that they want to be with me. You shouldn't either.

I know that a lot of women worry that playing hard to get is going to make a guy disappear. But try to think about it this way: Playing hard to get is a great way to put the guy to the test early on. If someone is truly interested in you, playing hard to get—or just going about your own damn life—won't deter them. And if it does? Then you've done yourself a favor and saved yourself some time. Plus, when the going gets tough—and it will, because no amount of manifestation can make real life go away—you don't want someone who disappears the second they have to put some work into the relationship.

RULE #7: KEEP YOUR OWN BANK ACCOUNT

Minding your money and minding your vagina are virtually the same when it comes to relationships—you have to protect your power. And it doesn't get any more powerful than the dollars in your pocketbook. Look, I want a sugar daddy as much as the next girl—I mean, why spend my money when I could spend his? I *chose* to be with someone who was independently wealthy. But I learned the hard way with Mr. V that by giving up my own income, I was also giving up my independence.

So, while I always wanted to have a rich husband, I knew that I needed to make my own money first. And that's exactly what I did—I made my first million on my own, before meeting Christian. Today, I spend my own money on all of the things that I buy. It's not that Christian doesn't offer. It's that I never want to say, "Oh, Daddy, may I please have this Gucci sweater?" I value being able to buy something for myself because I earned it. And I love not having to depend on someone else financially.

One of my lines from the show became notorious, when I joked that I like going shopping with my husband's credit card while he's sleeping and said, "Some call it fraud; I call it love." If

super smart—and I liked that we were both in the same phase of our lives. Being in your late twenties and dating in LA is kind of a funny phase because you end up meeting a lot of guys who have already been married or already have kids. But I wasn't interested in that kind of baggage. I was hoping to find someone like me—a person who had been so busy building their career that they hadn't found too much time to date. And that was Christian. Then, at the end of the night he asked if he could drive me home. Normally I'm pretty private about where I live because I've dated some pretty shady guys, so I declined and said I would take an Uber. But he was really insistent, and I wasn't getting ax murder vibes from him, so I let him drive me and had him drop me off at the corner. But once again he insisted on getting me home—in a kind, considerate way—so I let him walk me to my door. He was clearly so happy with how the date went, and it was refreshing to meet someone who was so transparent. He wasn't some LA guy trying to be someone he's not or constantly bragging about who he knows or what he does for a living (which is so many of the guys out here); he was a nerd. And if you remember me saying in Season 1, that's all I wanted—a nice, nerdy guy to balance me out. From that date on, Christian was so eager to spend time with me, and I loved that about him. It was always off-the-cuff and spontaneous, like "Let's go to Aspen!"—that's what he said to me after our first date. I'm like, I don't even know you! But it was sweet. And even though I did initially think, *OK, this guy needs some fucking work* and made him my *Queer Eye*-style project by styling him and insisting he grew some stubble on his face so that he didn't look like a 1970s rapist, it was eventually love.

HOW THE HELL DID CHRISTIAN RETIRE AT THIRTY-SEVEN?

My husband is the reason we have food delivery apps today! He was the first to create a food delivery platform while also running the company. And when other companies came along and tried to do the same thing, they couldn't compete. He also gained major notoriety as one of the first companies to accept bitcoin as a form of currency—a complete unknown back in 2013. At the time, if you could figure out how to buy one, it would have cost you $88. But Christian was able to see the potential for the currency to evolve and allowed people to use it for all fifteen thousand restaurants on his platform. This caught the media's attention overnight.

For a while, his company had a hold on the market and a huge fleet of drivers. Eventually, Grubhub made him an insane offer he couldn't refuse, just so it wouldn't have to compete anymore, like "Listen, we'll pay you just to go away." Christian never had a single investor, so by owning 100 percent of his company and then selling it, he made enough money to retire at thirty-seven.

But once our relationship got serious, I convinced him that he'd be bored doing nothing at such a young age. So he's back to working part-time in tech again. Being such a smart and curious person, he wouldn't be happy just lazing around all day with a glass of champs on the beach without some hard work in his life. That's just not the way he . . . or I! . . . was meant to live. The fun is in the hustle!

HOW DID CHRISTIAN PROPOSE?

Our proposal story was exactly what I wanted it to be. We were between houses at the time, so we were staying at the Hotel Bel-Air. We'd ordered room service, and he surprised me by asking, "Will you marry me?" over a club sandwich, a Dr Pepper, and a bottle of champagne. It was perfect. I didn't need the whole Kanye treatment—no shutting down a ballpark, no orchestra, no one else flown in for the occasion. I just wanted something simple and meaningful. He nailed it.

HOW DID YOU DECIDE TO HAVE A BABY?

We talked about having kids on our very first date, which is one of the reasons I think our relationship worked out as well as it did—we were so honest and open with each other about our goals from the very beginning. So we were definitely both on the same page. As far as the timing, I don't think either of us was prepared for things to happen as quickly as they did—after all, I'm the ultimate planner and usually need things nailed down to the very last detail, which is not exactly how nature operates—but I'm so glad it happened when it did. First of all, I think it's really easy to put things off and think you have all the time in the world, but I'm already thirty-three! If I had waited for everything in my life to be "perfect," I'd probably be seventy-five before I got around to having kids. But luckily by conceiving when I did, I was able to be pregnant during the COVID quarantine and then have the baby as the world was opening up just a little bit. I wouldn't have changed this non-plan plan for the world!

WHAT'S YOUR LIFE LIKE TOGETHER TODAY?

Our daily life is a lot like our proposal story, actually! We are a lot more normal than people realize. I think there's probably this misconception about Christian that he's a label-loving rich dude, à la Mr. Valentino, but he's actually the opposite. He doesn't care about flexing brand names whatsoever. I have bought him so many clothes and shoes, but he just wears the same, simple outfits over and over. Honestly, if you saw him walking down the street, you'd never guess that had a dime to his name. Legitimately. He just doesn't care about material things. But we do share a love of travel, and not just that—five-star travel to places like St. Barths, Bali, Bora Bora, and the Maldives. When we're not traveling, we are total homebodies. We'll sit by the pool, take a bath, read books, and just talk. Even before we were a boring married couple, we were a boring married couple! If we can spend a night at home nerding out, we'll do that over a night out almost every time.

We can talk about anything together. On any given day, you could find us discussing politics or philosophy. We don't actually like going out to dinner, so we will order in from Mastro's, this fabulous steakhouse where we had our first date. We love good food, but we prefer to eat it in our robes at home where we can be truly comfortable. Nearly every night before we go to bed, we read together. Sometimes he reads aloud to me, too, which is really sweet. We read all of Lauren Weisberger's books together and, lately, lots of baby sleep-training books. I'm so excited to watch Baby C grow up and continue bonding with my husband! Christian is already talking about everything he's going to teach our son on the computer. At this rate, Baby C is probably going to be hacking into the Pentagon by preschool.

I love that Christian and I are opposites in many ways, and I have the fabulous elements of my life to enjoy, and a husband who I love and relate to on a deep level at home with me every night. I know you can find the same for yourself, too.

CHAPTER 6

GET RICH AF

To be a Boss Bitch is to completely own your power. And if there's one thing that gives you more control than pretty much all of the other factors we've talked about in this book combined, it's money. Money *is* power. It's the ability to make your own choices; go where you want, when you want; walk out of a job that sucks; walk away from a relationship that sucks; and treat yourself whenever and however you want to. There's a reason why they call cash in the bank "Fuck You money." The minute I started getting smart about my finances was the moment I finally got into the driver's seat of my life. And bitch, you know that if I'm going to drive, then the whip's gotta be full-on European luxury. That's why I wanted to dedicate a chapter to the cold, hard currency that makes this world go 'round.

If you're going to be a Boss Bitch, then you have to get comfortable with money—how to save it, how to spend it, how to know your worth, and how to all around get what's yours. *But what if I just want to marry rich?* you say? OK, I see you. We'll also cover how to sugar daddy responsibly because I have the expert playbook for that, too. But spoiler alert, you still need to have your finances locked down because nothing spells disaster for a Boss Bitch more than having to beg Daddy for every last dime.

People assume that I came from a rich family. But call me Iggy Azalea because I started from the bottom and now I'm here. I didn't grow up in complete poverty, but my family had such a lack mindset. My mom scrimped and saved for everything. Either she made our clothes or we'd get them secondhand, and she was the coupon-clipping master. She could stretch leftovers for an entire week. And just like she parented from a place of No, that's how she approached life's small indulgences, too. It was always "We don't have the money to go to dinner"; "We can't do this; we can't do that." My parents were always talking about things that they didn't have. If we didn't have a coupon for it, it pretty much didn't happen. And it would drive me batty. I knew that I never wanted to live the ultraconservative life that my parents did, but when it came to money, it was more than just a lifestyle choice. The issue here wasn't about not having enough—because sometimes you do have to make tough choices in order to make ends meet, and that's just how it is. I wasn't upset with them about the fact that our clothes were never new or that we never really went on vacations, although certainly I dreamed of a life where I could have and do anything I wanted to. No, for me the problem was that their views about money were just an extension of how they were hiding from the world. As I saw it, money was freedom, but they were squandering every last bit that they had. They were too afraid to see that if they spent $30 once a month on a meal that we could all share and enjoy, it wouldn't be the difference between paying our mortgage and being homeless. They had embraced the antiquated mentality that you save and you save and you save and then you die. And to me, that wasn't living. So, from the time I was young, I started to get the idea that if I just changed my mindset about money, I could live more richly.

Around the time I started thinking about these things, I became friends with Amanda. Amanda was that chick I was telling you about a few chapters ago—she was a fellow loser like me, so the two of us hit it off. And our moms were friends, so I was actually allowed to hang out with her and sometimes, on special occasions, I'd get to sleep at her house. I loved spending time with Amanda because, in addition to knowing what it was like to be bullied by a bunch of high school assholes, she was also fucking loaded. As I mentioned before, her dad was the CEO of RadioShack, so that girl wanted for nothing. She was like Blair Waldorf. Well, one time when my mom was in the hospital, I was sent to stay at Amanda's house for an entire week—which under normal circumstances would never have been permitted. To make it an even bigger deal, during that time, her dad was going to be on a business trip to New York, and Amanda and her mom were planning to go with him. And somehow, miraculously, my parents said that I could go, too.

We stayed at this gorgeous hotel with a big glass staircase that I can still picture so clearly because it made such an impression on me, and Amanda and I had an enormous suite all to ourselves. We were zipping in and out of department stores like Bergdorf Goodman, Barneys, and Bendel's, where Amanda's mom told us that we could get anything we wanted. It was crazy to me at the time, being able to pick out a $37 Chanel lip gloss—like, who would pay that much for that? (Unfortunately, me now, on the regular.) Her parents got us a reservation at Britney Spears's brand-new restaurant, Nyla, and then let us take our own limo around the city. We were sixteen years old, drinking champagne, hanging our heads out of the sunroof as we sang Britney Spears songs at the top of our lungs, living our best fucking lives.

It was one thing for me to have seen this kind of wealth in my hometown in Texas, but here in the bustle of New York, watching all these women on the sidewalk just turned out and looking amazing with their fresh Sally Hershberger blowouts and Miuccia Prada knee-high crocodile boots, it was completely eye-opening for me. I'd never experienced this kind of luxury and glamour firsthand—and it was everything I wanted when I grew up. I thought, *I don't know how, and I don't care how, but one day, I'm going to have all this.* My eyes were now completely open to the fact that if I was going to stay trapped in my parents' house doing my best Rapunzel impression, then I was never going to get anywhere. And the key to unlocking that door was money.

Then and there I knew that if I was going to start building the life that I wanted and knew that I deserved, I was going to have to go out and start making my own money. At first that meant taking any job I could get, in my case at places like Sonic and Taco Bell. I didn't get too hung up on the fact that these weren't be-all and end-all of jobs; they paid well enough. And because I was living with my parents, I could save everything that I made. I may have disagreed with my dad about a lot of things, but I always respected him because he's very, very smart, and the one thing he always drilled into me was how important it was to save. Specifically, he told me to save a minimum of 20 percent of my paycheck. So every single paycheck that came in, 20 percent of it would go into savings and the other 80 percent I could spend on whatever I wanted. But as tempting as it was to go out and blow all that money on clothes, it was more important to me to build a safety net for the day that I would eventually move out. The only thing I wanted more than to leave was to not have to come back a failure. I wanted to prove to my parents that I wasn't a fuckup. So even when I was pursuing my dream job of becoming an actress or a model, I always had another job that could pay the bills.

Eventually I got a job at a bar, which was another fantasy of mine because I always wanted to be a bartender like you see in the movies—the sassy, doesn't-give-a-fuck bitch who runs the place, makes drink orders with one hand, and rips a shot of whiskey, Coyote Ugly–style, with the other. I also knew that they made a lot of money. So I doctored my resume (we're talking worthy of an honorary MD), lied about my age—because Texas was the Wild West back then and employers didn't ask you for jack shit when you applied for a job—and got the gig. I'd be making a cash hourly and then my tips. Well, my first night I made about $300. I was making that at Sonic in a week. It was a lot of fucking money. But also, I worked hard for it. It wasn't like I sat back and hoped to make 20 percent of the bar tab. No, I'd be out there chatting people up, being their therapist, having fun with them. I knew that acting would come in handy in business, trying out characters and all that, and it was especially true with bartending. When I saw it literally pay off in my first paycheck, it instantly clicked: I was in control of this ride.

After years and years of feeling like I had no power at all, this was one of the moments that made me realize that I really did have the ability to go out into the world and make my own way with what eventually became my signature Boss Bitch hustle. And not only that, whatever cash I did manage to make was my ticket to anywhere that I wanted to go. And I set my sights on the tippy fucking top. People ask me all the time why I still work even though I married a wealthy man. It's because I get so much satisfaction out of being able to do things for myself. This is what I worked so hard to achieve: being able to work on my own terms, do my own thing, and know that I can always fend for myself. Plus, the extra spending money (aka Sephora credits) doesn't hurt either. I have a strong work ethic—not something I was born with, but something that I acquired over time, as you can too—and feel fulfilled and whole when I'm doing something that I feel passionate about, so I love working and I always will. But mostly, I think there's something so powerful about not needing a man but *choosing* to have one. Because as smart as I'd been with money my whole life, I'd found a habit of putting myself in situations where I needed to rely on someone else, and I never wanted to feel that way again.

Take Mr. Valentino. My life with him was straight off my manifestation board—the Louboutins, the clothes, the fabulous trips on the Gulfstreams. But he wanted me to quit my job at the bar. At first, I was hesitant to do it. I'd learned how incredibly freeing it was to be making my own money. And while it wasn't as though I was making millions and I'd be lucky to make $2,000 a month, that was still $2,000 a month that was completely mine. But he was as persistent, as his bank account was abundant, and then he got more and more manipulative. He'd say things like "I'd really like to take you on this trip, but I guess you'll have to check with work first." Or "We could travel so much more if you'd just quit." He appealed to the side of me that wanted to be taken care of, which I mean, don't we all? And I didn't have the balls to deny him that. I also conveniently ignored the red flag that the relationship probably wouldn't have worked out if I'd kept that job. And so even though I had this gorgeous man and was living in his gorgeous house and leading this first-class super-luxe life, I was missing the most important thing—freedom. According to him, my friends were never good enough. He would tell me how they were all such losers, that he didn't know why I hung out with them, and that it was honestly just embarrassing for me to be seen with them. Slowly, my girls' nights, my acting classes, my hobbies, my time with my family, and my friends faded away. And it wasn't because they were "losers"—these people were vibrant and confident—he just wanted to phase everyone out of my life. If I wanted to do something or buy something, he'd insist on coming with me. To go to dinner with my friends, the grocery store, to get a fucking cup of coffee at Starbucks—he'd have to come because he'd give me an ultimatum: I go or you don't get the cash. I'd try pushing back and telling him that he couldn't just be my walking pocketbook, but because I thought I needed him more than I needed my independence, I didn't want to push him too far and risk losing him. It was a classic Power of the Pussy teachable moment: I was afraid to ask, so I got nothing. And I definitely hadn't yet figured out my worth. When I eventually broke up with him, I knew that I would never, ever put myself in a position like that again.

This chapter is the product of all the lessons that I learned in order to create full-on financial independence for myself. So, while I may not be some kind of financial expert with a briefcase and fancy letters after my name, I can tell you with no hesitation that just a few simple tools and rules of thumb are to credit for my success. The beauty of these tools is that they're available to anyone, anytime, at any age, in any tax bracket. It doesn't matter if you work three jobs just to make ends meet or you're a hedge fund power bitch; the same rules apply and the same rules will pay off. If money is the passport to get the life you want, no matter what that may look like, a combination of hustle, common sense, and keeping your eyes on the motherfucking prize is going to get you rich AF. Let's go make it rain, bitches.

HOW TO SAVE

People are always asking me how I made all my money. Besides be a certified hustler, I'd have to say that the number-one secret is learning how to save. I know that when you saw this chapter was about getting rich, you were hoping for some kind of map across the rainbow to the pot of gold, but I can promise you that if you can learn how to save, then you can make your money work double-time no matter how much or how little you make—although I do think there's always room for improvement in the income department . . . but we'll get to that in a moment.

As I mentioned earlier, saving a piece of my paycheck every single time is a lesson I learned from my dad. From my first job at Sonic, I made a habit of setting aside 20 percent of anything I earned, *minimum*. I know it sounds stupid simple, but so many people get a paycheck for $2,000 and think they have $2,000. But you don't. You have rent, utilities, car payments, gas, groceries. All that fun stuff. So there's income and then there's discretionary income, or the amount that's left after you've taken out everything else that needs to be paid or else you're out on your ass in the street.

As I made more money as a model and actress, and eventually as a real estate agent, that 20 percent was still consistently getting set aside. Sometimes it would be more if I was feeling extra-mature or was saving up for a specific goal like a new car or a bigger apartment—but never, ever less. In hindsight, I wish I had regularly upped that amount to 30 or even 40 percent and made myself more money (especially after I started investing, which we'll talk about in just a sec). But when you work hard, you want to spend some of that 80 percent on yourself. So you know what? YOLO. Though, like I said, that 20 percent is non-negotiable, so no matter what you do, don't skimp on that.

GET BITCHY

Something that helped me keep track of my finances, especially when I was just starting to earn money, was to write everything down. First of all, that's because I'm very visual and seeing things on paper feels much more real to me. It's why I don't do anything on my phone; I keep track of everything in my agenda or write it all out in a journal. I mean, I still mail out checks. When I write down actual, specific dollar amounts, I can see the cold, hard facts about what I need to save for and exactly how much money I have. It's a lot harder to play games when the numbers are staring you in the face. This exercise is the perfect combo of financial planning and goal setting. And you'll also see that it's a lot like vision boarding, which we're going to spend the next chapter talking about (because dreaming big and manifesting it to happen is *everything*).

What I want you to do is make a list of every expense that you have to pay every month. So there's your rent, your car payment, your utilities, maybe school tuition. And then add in the other smaller things that you know you're going to be spending on, too, like gas, groceries, and dry cleaning. Do your best to estimate on these. If it's helpful, look back at the past couple months of credit card statements to see what they've been on average. Don't cut corners here—the more you include, the better idea you're going to have of how much money you really need to be setting aside every month. Believe me, I know it's not the most fun to have to do this, but what did you think getting your money in order was going to look like? You can't be making it rain if you don't get your shit together first.

Now that you have your list, I want you to add up all those numbers. The resulting amount is your do-or-die, need-to-nail-it goal every month. The 20 percent that you're pulling from each paycheck is going to cover that first. But here's the thing—anything left over from the 20 percent once you've paid for every single thing on that list is *not* fun money. No, girl. That money stays in your savings. Do you hear me? I didn't just get where I am financially today because I made bank and married well. A big piece of my success is that money that I saved every single month. So don't sleep on your savings.

Now this next bit is crucial: Every month I want you to track your spending and your savings. I want you to write down everything in that standing-expense category so you can see how that 20 percent is being spent and how much is left over. From month to month, hopefully you'll see that number grow. But you're not going to just sit back and wait for that little sapling of a number to grow into a big-ass tree. No, you're going to throw some turbo-charged fertilizer on that shit. And the way you're going to do that is this: Pick a goal.

I'm a major believer that setting a goal is one of the best ways to align your mind and your actions, which I'll be teaching in the next chapter. For now, suffice it to say that by picking out something that you want to save up for, you'll be giving purpose to this whole ordeal. And while, yeah, you could make that goal a pair of shoes or new jewelry, I'm encouraging you to dig a little deeper. What would be a game-changer for you? A down payment on a house? A car? A laptop? A class or training that would get you closer to your dream job? Just make sure that it's achievable—I know I told you to dream big, but wishing for a $10 million house out of the gate is a little lofty and is only going to make you frustrated. And then every month, when you see your savings, ask yourself if you're on track to hitting your goal in a reasonable amount of time. If not, you're going to do one of two things (or both, if you really want to know what I think):

1. You're going to start regularly contributing more to your little nest egg. I know it's not always easy to choose savings or sushi, but be honest with yourself—how bad do you want to hit that goal? And wouldn't it be amazing if it happened in the next few years and not twenty years from now?

2. You're going to think about boosting the amount of money you make in the first place. If you're in a position to do so, can you challenge yourself to make more next month and the month after that? Can you ask your boss for that long-overdue raise that you know you deserve but just haven't gotten the balls to discuss? As you'll see a little later in this chapter, recognizing your worth—and demanding that others recognize it, too—is one of the essential keys to boosting your net worth.

INVESTING

I'm not here to pull a Leo in *Wolf of Wall Street*—I'm not going to tell you what exactly to do with your money—but I can recommend that you take the time to get educated about where you're parking the money that you're setting aside. Because the next level of saving is investing, or having your money start to work for you. And by that I mean earning more interest while it just sits and waits patiently for you to come and spend it on your fabulous goal. I know for some of you just setting aside money in the first place makes you get *Great Gatsby* vibes, but there's no reason to settle for that Bank of America account earning you 1 percent interest when you could be earning more in your sleep.

I started investing my money when I was eighteen years old. I opened an account at TD Ameritrade and then opened an investment account. I learned that I could deposit the money that I wanted to put aside, essentially forget about it, and ultimately watch it grow without me having to lift a finger. And because in a lot of cases you can't move your money for a certain period of time, it meant that I didn't start itching to get my paws on those funds for something that I knew I shouldn't be spending it on. Because as good as I was at saving, I'm still human, and an extra $1,000 just sitting in a checking account would have probably made its way toward a new bag. That's the beauty of having a savings account in general—you'll never be able to play that game of "knowing" how much money you can spend; it's there in your account balance in black and white. When it comes to investing and setting money aside, there is a clear winner: US public index funds. But this comes with a huge caveat: You must promise yourself not to let emotions take over. Investing is a long game, and the real earnings happen when you hang in there, through both the ups and the downs of the market. There will be headlines about the impending doom of a crash. Some of these headlines will play out, and, furthermore, there is an absolute certainty that the value of your investments will decline at times. Do you have the emotional fortitude not to sell during these times? Do you have the confidence to politely ignore the advice of people who are fearful of the stock market?

Also, pay close attention to the fees associated with your investments. A 2 percent annual fee might not sound like much, but over the course of your life, it adds up to a huge number because of the compounding effect over time.

If there is a single strategy to adopt, it is to invest a portion of your income every month, through thick and thin. This is called "dollar cost averaging," and it works. Experiment with online interest calculators. The US S&P 500 has consistently returned an average of 9.7 percent annually. This is an average, and therefore comes with rocky times along the way. It can, and almost surely will, drop substantially for short periods along the way. But, just as surely as it will drop, it will quickly rebound stronger than ever. Take a look at the charts to prove it to yourself. Pay attention to what happened after every decline. Now, imagine your savings right before a decline. Can you handle seeing the drop that comes next without selling? If so, you can be sure that you'll win over the course of your life.

Can you afford to put aside $250 each month into a low-cost S&P 500 index fund? If so, by adopting this strategy, you're likely to have half a million dollars in 30 years.

When it comes to investing and setting money aside, what's most important is that you don't invest anything that you can't afford to lose. Especially if you're dealing with stocks, that's not where you want your life savings to go. But if you have a couple thousand that you're hanging on to for a rainy day without super-high stakes, work with your financial advisor to figure out your goals, your timeline, and how much risk you're willing to take.

NEVER PAY RETAIL

On a more day-to-day, cash-in-my-wallet level, I've found other ways to save money. I do love to shop, and it's no secret that I have expensive taste, but I'm actually super careful about how I choose to spend. So, when I do want to splurge, I always do it intelligently. Which is where never paying retail comes in. I first figured this out when I wanted to make my first big purchase after making money in real estate. I'd had a rose-gold Daytona Rolex on my vision board for years, and it was finally time to make that manifestation come true. Because I had been putting aside 20 percent religiously, I wanted to reward myself with a tangible reminder of my success. But I wasn't about to walk into a store and pay retail for this $75,000 watch. Hell no. I'm not stupid with my money. So instead, I went to consignment store. I'd been selling stuff there for a while because I had so many shoes that Mr. Valentino had bought me that couldn't fit in my apartment anymore, and I knew that there were lots of other people like me who'd gotten really special items as gifts or maybe needed to clean out their closets and so were sending their things to the site. I started browsing for the watch, and sure enough, I found the exact same one for $25,000, a third of the price of a brand-new one. And yet this one was in perfect condition—it just happened to be owned by someone else. It was so exciting because I was able to buy myself something I'd wanted for a long time; I could wear it every single day; and it would never go out of style. It wasn't any less special to me because I'd found this crazy good deal—in fact, it made me feel smart. And it was aligned with my goal of wanting to continue building my wealth, which I'd never be able to do if I dropped a hundred grand every time I wanted to treat myself.

I was also very into this scenario because it taught me about depreciating assets and assets that maintain their value. It's important to realize when you're spending your hard-earned money that there are some things that lose their value and others that maintain it. The reality is, those gorgeous Brian Atwood pumps start losing value the second you walk them out of the store. That Cartier Love bracelet, on the other hand, that's financially timeless. In most cases, unless you're buying couture, your clothes and shoes aren't forever buys. Jewelry and diamonds, in addition to being a girl's best friend, are investments.

The other lesson here is what you're really spending your money on when you walk into a store. Take diamonds, for example. I'd started taking an interest in them when Mr. Valentino would take me to Tiffany's and Cartier and buy me little things like necklaces and bracelets, and I'd mentally take note of the price. Then I would go onto sites like Blue Nile to look at stones and learn about things like color, clarity, inclusions, cut, and sizing. What I realized is that diamonds are essentially a dime a dozen but places like Tiffany's purchase them and mark them up, sometimes as much as four times their actual value.

Then one day we were in Van Cleef & Arpels. I pointed out a necklace I thought was sweet and the saleswoman told me it was $12,000. Twelve thousand dollars for a few microscopic diamonds and some mother of pearl?! I was blown away. I couldn't believe that people were paying this much for a stone that doesn't come out of the ground stamped with "Harry Winston." Your diamonds aren't more special because of their name brand; you're just paying more for them because you don't know the jewelry game . . . yet. I love when girls are showing off their rings saying, "It's 4 karats!" Well, guess what, bitch, you could have had double that for the same price, if your daddy did his research. My friend who is a diamond dealer verified my apprehension about how you don't have to spend that much on a stone. Her advice to me was this: Always buy from a GIA-certified wholesale diamond dealer or trusted resale sites such as the RealReal or 1stDibs. Never retail. Also, buy the best quality diamonds that you can with the budget you have. That's because not all diamonds are created equal. Get familiar with the four Cs: carat, color, clarity, and cut because each of these attributes affect how valuable your stone is. It might surprise you to hear that the size of the diamond is actually less important than the color and clarity when it comes to holding value—that's right, my loves, bigger is not always better. But of course, there are those huge, fabulous diamonds with great color and clarity that are super rare—those you never sell. You collect them!

Now that you're looking to save money, think about how you can shop smarter, too. Consider sites like the RealReal instead of buying things straight from the store. I know how fun it can be to come out of Barneys with all your bags doing your best Julia Roberts down Rodeo, but you're not just paying for that blazer or trousers or dress when you do that. You're paying the markup from wholesale, the markup for the brand or designer name, the markup for the store's name, and then the sales tax (8.25 percent here in California). I don't know about you, honey, but I work way too hard for my money to be lighting it on fire like that. (I'll save those gas cans for an ex's house.)

HOW TO SPEND

Growing up seeing my parents live this dreary life of restraint and sacrifice, I knew that I wanted to find a different relationship with my money. I'd gotten the saving part down cold, but what about the rest of it? What was the point of working my ass off if I couldn't enjoy the fruits of my labor? If I wasn't seeing the value of what money could do for me or the happiness that it could make me feel, then what was I really even working for? I wasn't about to go out and toss around all my hard-earned cash because the stakes were way too high—I *had* to make it on my own no matter what—but like I said, I wanted to live with a little, you know, *sparkle*.

The first thing I had to do was retrain my brain to believe that I could afford things and that it was OK to spend money. I didn't know it at the time, but this was one of my early manifesting exercises—the more I believed I could spend, the more money I made to cover those expenses. It might sound simplistic, but it's a very powerful exercise and motivator. Because the more I enjoyed spending my money, the more incentivized I was to earn more.

The first time I tried this out was when I was working as a model, doing mostly boring commercial print work. But I got paid $1,500 a day, which for me at the time was crazy money. Like, over a thousand dollars just for being on set and having fun? To me, this was Gwen Stefani b-a-n-a-n-a-s. I set aside my usual 20 percent and my agent's commission, but I still had all this money left. I was tempted to put all of it into savings because there was nothing that I needed-needed, but then my imagination started going about what I could possibly spend that money on. And wasn't that the point? To make money so that I could actually enjoy it?? At first I thought I'd buy some new clothes, but I was always wearing them once and returning them (another trick I've used throughout my life, especially when I was going on dates and shooting the first season of the show, but you didn't hear it from me!). Then I thought about beauty products, which I'd had a fascination with ever since I started shoplifting eyeliner from the drugstore as a preteen. (Side note life hack: Sephora has a kick-ass return policy and will even take returns of *fully used* makeup if you simply "didn't like it." Just *beep boop beep*; money back.) So I decided to take myself to Nordstrom and went counter by counter—La Prairie, Chanel, YSL. I ended up buying some new products and a couple red lipsticks, which I could never have enough of. Because I was buying quality items that I genuinely loved, I not only made myself supremely happy but I also felt like I was investing in myself. I wasn't worried about the splurge because I knew I could afford it, and it made me even more amped up to go out and earn more money next month so I could do it all over again. Over time, I also got the hang of what I wanted to spend my money on, which were things I could enjoy over and over again, like shoes and bags, versus chipping away at that 80 percent with a bunch of silly, throwaway purchases.

<u>GET BITCHY</u>

The next time you get paid, take out your planner once again and do your regular savings exercise. Put aside that 20 percent and any other expenses that need to come out. Rookie mistake alert: Don't forget to also account for the money that you will need to put aside for taxes. Then look at what's left—that's your play money. That's yours to *Parks and Rec*-style "treat yo self." Ask yourself what would feel meaningful and lasting beyond just blowing it on something you won't even remember in a week. Think about items, services, or experiences that would make you feel really appreciated for all the work that went into earning this money. For me, I always valued my extensive and overly excessive nightly bedtime routine. In addition to my silk pillowcase and eye mask that I have never been able to live without, there is something so luxe-feeling about slathering myself in a totally over-the-top nine-step regimen of overpriced potions and lotions. Every night I would go to bed feeling rich AF. I felt Like an Upper East Sider named Caroline who came from money, summered in the Hamptons, and wore diamonds in the ocean. Little things like this trained my brain to make me believe I was *that* rich. Spend your money on things that make you feel *that* good.

That said, not every month needs to be a shopping spree, and I don't recommend you spend every last penny of that 80 percent. Not to be a total downer, but shit happens—we know this. If every month you're ending up with a ton left over and going out of your way to look for things to spend it on, consider upping how much you're contributing to your savings. Could you get to 30 percent? Forty? Then ramp up your savings goal to sweeten the deal.

HOW TO NEGOTIATE

Real estate is only worth what someone is willing to pay. Just like real estate, remember that everything in life can always be negotiated. I will always remember my first deal as a real estate agent. I had gone to an open house and met this woman who was a fashion designer and ran this huge fashion company, and I was so excited to meet her because I actually owned a few of her dresses. She was looking for a real estate agent and said, "You seem sophisticated and smart, will you help me find a house?" And even though I was just starting out and getting a feel for the job, I told her that I would happily represent her. She had no idea that I was new because I was faking it so hard it hurt (Boss Bitch Business Rule #2), acting like I'd been doing it for years, and besides, I knew that I was going to totally kill it. But what caught me off guard was all the lying that would happen when trying to negotiate with the other agents. It would be no secret that a house had been sitting on the market for 132-plus days or had fallen out of escrow, and yet here were these other agents being majorly shady. Or when my client had finally found a house she loved, the seller's agent called and was like "I just want to let you know that an offer came in last night for over asking, all cash." Bull fucking shit. We knew that this house had been sitting forever and that they were just trying to play games, but my client freaked out because at the end of the day, she really wanted the house. So I said to her, "I need you to trust me on this. This isn't real. We're not putting in an offer because we're going to call their bluff." I knew what this house meant to my client, but I also wasn't about to let this agent turn the tables on us—he needed to sell the house more than we needed to buy it. I also knew that if there was another offer, which there obviously wasn't but still, we could come in higher or ask for more favorable terms like a fourteen-day or seven-day close with no contingencies. Because I knew my shit. Sure enough, the agent called me a few days later, saying, "Oh my gosh, that crazy offer we had fell through, blah blah blah." I said to him, "Don't bullshit with me, there was never an offer. And if we're going to do business, rule number one is you don't lie to me." He was shocked that I was talking to him like that, but I stood my ground because I was right and he knew it. I also held all the cards—I had all the leverage. Like I said on the show, I can Bobby Fischer the shit out of any situation; I'm always thinking eight steps ahead.

Whether it's in business or in life, finding your leverage is everything. Once you know your value and what you have to offer—and how that's more than anyone else can offer in a certain situation—it becomes a lot easier to get what you want. That could be a raise, a better price on a car, a better price on a house, or better terms in a contract. That's why I recommend taking a minute before a negotiation to write down on paper what you bring to the table. Say, "Here's what I'm good at; here's what I can deliver; these are my strengths; these are my attributes." That way you can stick to your guns and never waver. It's also important to take that time to figure out what that other person needs in order to feel whole and what their pressure points might be. Maybe that car salesperson needs to hit their numbers by the end of the month. Or you know your company can't afford to lose another person on your team.

And I recommend being prepared to walk away if a situation isn't going to give you what you want and deserve. When you truly know your worth, then you'll know when an offer doesn't match up to that. And that's exactly what will become your leverage—that you're prepared to leave the table if it comes down to it. Even though it sounds strange, that's actually a very powerful position to take in a negotiation. Because when you're prepared to leave with nothing, then you feel empowered to ask for everything. And above all, trust your gut. If something doesn't feel right, then it probably isn't.

HOW TO SUGAR DADDY

We can't talk about the quest for cash without addressing one of the oldest forms of investments that women have made in their future: the Sugar Daddy. Though, it's important to point out that when I talk about sugar daddies here, it's with the full realization that a Sugar Mommy is equally beneficial for the bottom line. No matter which flavor you prefer, I can't deny that the right relationship can be the perfect diversification for your portfolio. And there's absolutely nothing wrong with that. I mean, let's be honest, there are some girls who love a man or woman with money in the bank. Who can blame them? There's something really sexy about someone with drive and business savvy; someone who knows what they want and goes out and grabs it; someone who still lives by the chivalry code and sees it as their duty to take care of the woman they're with. It's called Big Dick Energy for a reason! One of my first serious relationships, with Mr. Valentino, was a First-Class Sugar Daddy Experience. He got to have a beautiful woman on his arm, and I got to learn amazing life lessons from an older man while being relentlessly spoiled. But as much as we loved spending time together and took on the world like a modern-day Bonnie and Clyde (without all the bank robbing), it wasn't all Bentleys and Bottega. His money, which was initially the frosting on top of a relationship with a gorgeous man, became more like a weapon that he used to control me. Because I was young and naive, I allowed Mr. V to chip away at my power until the relationship became completely imbalanced. Out of fear that I would lose him, I let him convince me to leave my job so that I had to become completely dependent on him. As a result, I gave up a part of myself, too. That's why I wanted to impart this wisdom: If you're going to sugar daddy, you need to do it responsibly. And you do that by following this golden rule: **Spend His Money but Make Your Own.**

Accept all the gifts, go on all the trips; fuck, get your rent paid—but do not, under any circumstances, give up the one thing that puts some cash in your pocket every week. I don't care if you leave your corporate position as HBIC to sell beaded friendship bracelets to your rich friends in your spare time, or if you scale your shifts back from full-time to a couple a week—it doesn't matter what you do so long as you can make enough money to cover at least some of your expenses. There's no magic number here in terms of how much you need to be making; you'll know it's the sweet spot when you don't have to go begging for an allowance any time you want a cup of coffee. Maintaining that little bit of independence will do wonders not only for your own self-esteem but for your relationship as well. It will be your way of saying that there's no price tag for you and your time and that kind of unattainability—which to a man or woman who believes that everything has a price—is pure catnip. Meow to the Pussy Power.

As for anyone who feels like they need to throw shade at your sugar daddy arrangement—don't listen to that noise. All relationships are based on qualities that you find attractive about someone, whether it's their looks, their personality, or some other It-factor that really gets you going. So there's no reason why it should be out of the question that money be one of them. No one thinks twice if you date a fugly guy who has a great sense of humor! So if keys to the Benz is your love language, do you! Just remember that while clothes, shoes, and trips on the PJ can be bought, you can't be. Never let money make up for things that make you unhappy or uncomfortable, and definitely never let it change who you are. They're called sugar daddies for a reason— they should make life sweet.

CHAPTER 7

MANIFEST YOUR DESTINY

I've always considered myself a modern-day *bruja*. I've always had "powers" that I could never quite explain. It was as if my obsession with Sarah Jessica Parker in *Hocus Pocus* was starting to brew a theme in my life. No, seriously—I've always been able to make the impossible-at-the-time happen, and so can you. I would imagine the life that I wanted, even when it was so dramatically different from the life that I had, and ultimately, I got it. Growing up, I never had new clothes much less anything designer; I lived in a modest, simple home in a modest, simple neighborhood and was surrounded by people who worked the same nine-to-5, Dolly Parton–style, job their whole lives until they retired. I always knew that I wanted more. While other people my age were obsessing over petty school drama and living in their small, lame high school world, I was aching for bigger, bolder, more glitz, and more glam. Since I dreamed of becoming an actress in Hollywood, I would spoon-feed myself a steady diet of movies starring the baddest bitches of all time—Marilyn, Audrey, and Elizabeth. They'd enter a room, hair perfectly set, makeup on point, dripping in diamonds, draped in silk and fur. They didn't just walk, they glided, sauntered, and swayed against the backdrop of opulent homes or ritzy restaurants, champagne coupes resting comfortably in their freshly manicured hands. Men were defenseless against that kind of megawatt Pussy Power. I wanted *in*. And spoiler alert: It happened.

Way before Rhonda Byrne unleashed *The Secret*, I was realizing my own magic and attracting things into my own life. It made me realize that if you think it and believe it, it will come to you. Aka manifesting. You might think this is all a little too "woo," but I eat that shit up like the lobster and caviar I always used to order on every first date. Because it fucking works. That yacht I introduced you to in the first chapter? That image had prime real estate on my vision board the year before. My *Vogue* cover? Same thing. Not to mention fabulous trips I've taken to places like Indonesia, Bora Bora, and Fiji; regular jaunts on a private jet; and a fairy-tale wedding to an incredible man.

I'll never forget one of the first things I manifested—a Louis Vuitton purse. I'd always had expensive taste, and there was nothing I wanted more than a butter-soft leather bag with that unmistakable logo. By the time I turned eighteen, I decided I had to have one. But working as a bartender, I wasn't even close to being able to afford it. At this point I had about two thousand dollars to my name—coincidentally the exact amount the bag I was eyeing cost—but I needed that money for all the mature things like rent and the Whataburgers from the 99-cent menu that I was living on at the time. But you know what? I went to the Louis Vuitton store anyway.

I figured if I couldn't afford the bag, then the next best thing would be to "borrow "it. My plan was to buy the purse, take it for a test drive, then return it. I just wanted to see what it would feel like to own one, just get a little taste of life with all the luxurious trimmings. I brought the bag home and put it in my closet and on my kitchen counter. I stared at it every second I could for every single one of the fourteen days I had it before I needed to return it. I didn't know it, but I was already working the powerful steps of manifesting—imagining what you want to be yours and acting as if that's already the case.

When I'd run out of time with "my" bag, I brought it back to the store. To my horror, the bitchy employee told me there was a water stain on it and that he would not accept it nor refund my money. There was no water stain. He was fucking with me because he knew I'd bought it without any intention of keeping it. He was flat-out refusing to let me make the return. Being just eighteen, I didn't see any other option but to take the bag and go. I got back in my Ford Focus, placed the purse next to me on the passenger seat, and panicked. Rent was due and I had bills to pay. My bank account was literally in the double digits. I had always been great with money, knowing what I could and could not afford. For the first time ever, I fucked up. Big time. *What was I supposed to do now?*

Work at the bar was slow, as usual. I had a few regulars who would sit and complain to me—wife troubles, women troubles, lack of women troubles, the usual. As pathetic as it was, though, I enjoyed their company. It helped pass the time. Although, like clockwork, every night that month I was depressed, distraught, and drunk. I would down shot after shot, just to get through my shifts, knowing that the end of the month was coming up and it would be only a matter of days before there would be an eviction notice stamped on my door. My entire neighborhood was about to find out just how pathetic my life really was.

While serving up another round of lemon drops and Coors Light one night, the bar doors swung open to reveal a group of loud, rowdy, already-drunk people. Music to my ears—and my pocketbook. Madonna's "Like a Prayer" began playing in my mind, as if these people were here to save me from my financial sins. Drunk people who like to throw their money around are every bartender's dream, and mine was about to come true. The group ordered Cristal and Louis XIII Cognac plus Cuban cigar after Cuban cigar. They partied for hours and hours, as I tried to mentally tally how much I'd land as a tip. I figured it would at least be a few hundred dollars given the high-ticket items they were guzzling like water and sending up in smoke. It wouldn't be enough to cover the rent, but I figured maybe I could work out a deal with my landlord. When it was time for last call, I handed someone in the group the bill, he handed it back, and my draw dropped. This man tipped me two thousand dollars on the dot. Exactly what I needed to cover the purse. I'd never received a tip like that in my life. Not even close. But on that particular night, I believed—and still do—that I made that purse mine with a combination of manifestation and hard work. And if it worked with one little bag, what else could I manifest?

Years ago, Jason Oppenheim and I secured the listing on a fabulous house with an even more fabulous client. Crystal Hefner, Hugh's last wife, had been the owner since he passed in 2017; it was the last piece of real estate he ever purchased. You could just picture Crystal on the property, sunbathing on a raft in nothing but a skimpy string bikini, long blonde hair cascading out of her ponytail and skimming the water, a glass of Whispering Angel in hand. But make no mistake: This is not the picture of a gold-digging bimbo. Crystal was, in fact, a fellow Boss Bitch herself. She was using the property as a rental while living in a much more modest home and saving the rental income. (Hopefully at least 20 percent, per my CQ Guide to Getting Rich AF.)

And the house was stunning. Floor-to-ceiling glass windows wrapped around this modern anything-but-humble abode. I had to make it mine. But how? At the time, I was barely scraping by, barely able to pay rent. I was juggling a handful of clients, but at this point had not yet closed on a property. In real estate, the biggest misconception is that we are paid a salary. But you don't make a single dollar unless you produce. And despite me desperately spinning my wheels and hustling as hard as I could, I wasn't there yet. I had even reined in my ego and started taking on rental properties, just to create a consistent (tiny, trickling) stream of income. So at this point, buying the house was just about as far-fetched as selling it—which I was determined to do.

I would sit as this property for open houses every Sunday and Tuesday from one P.M. to four P.M. for months on end. But instead of getting hung up on how long it was taking and how much of my schedule it was eating up, I decided to put that time to work. I made that house mine; I made it my bitch. Every minute that I sat there, I'd imagine myself living in these rooms. I'd perch on the couch and could practically see my as-yet-nonexistent husband, shirtless and jogging down the stairs, espresso in hand. I remember twirling around in the closet thinking, *How in the hell am I supposed to fit all of my shoes in here?* For a nearly 7,000-square-foot house, the closet was proportionally insulting. It would be one of the first things I would fix before I even moved in, and I thought up changes to the floor plan that I would review with my architect over chopped salads at La Scala. I would use the bedroom to answer phone calls and write emails, just as if it were my very own bedroom. In my mind, it might as well have been.

Every time I closed up for the day and walked out of the property, I would check the mail for Crystal and leave it on the counter. But seeing her name on the letters in the kitchen of the house that I wished was my own was too jarring for the mental picture I was trying to create. So one day, before a private showing, I decided to take my own mail to Crystal's property to get some work done and pay some bills. Then boom, I had my first "aha" moment: That was the piece that was missing! I was doing everything I could to manifest the house, but by just sitting inside and pretending, I was really no better than a party crasher at best, stalker at worst. If I was going to get serious about manifesting this house, then I was going to have to put my stamp on it somehow, really trick my brain into believing that this was where I lived. A simple as it sounds, I started leaving my own mail on the counter. I was the only one regularly coming and going, so it wouldn't bother anyone, and I'd just clean up before showings. But when I'd walk in to set up, I'd drop my keys next to my stack of bills and issues of *Harper's*, *Us Weekly*, and *Vogue*. Honey, I'm home! I continued this routine for months until the listing eventually expired, despite all of our efforts to sell it. It was the end of my real estate fantasy . . . or so I thought.

Fast-forward to 2019. Christian (my then-fiancé) and I were attending the annual ice polo match at Badrutt's Palace Hotel in Switzerland. Without a home of our own at the time, we were drifters. We bounced between hotels and my two-bedroom apartment in Beverly Hills while we waited for something to catch our eye on the housing market. As you can imagine, after all those years of selling some of LA's most desirable houses, and me being, well, me, I wouldn't settle for anything less than perfect. We were flying back to the States when I got an email notification ding from my phone that there was a new listing to see. I had created an auto notification for houses that matched our criteria, and this one was a standout. A modern gated home, encased in glass, complete with a full pull-up motor court with enough space for ten cars—noteworthy because in LA, it's rare to even find a garage, let alone space for one or two cars. And the price was an absolute steal. I knew we had to see it immediately after we landed.

Walking up to the house groggy and jet-lagged, I shuffled through the front door and my mouth dropped open. This was the exact same home I used to sit inside for months on end, trying to sell it, wishing it was mine. I hadn't noticed it from the listing because the staging was so different. Being inside now, it was unmistakable. Everything I had visualized so intensely for years had come true.

But I'm not just lucky, and I didn't get any of this by magic. And I'm definitely not suggesting that you can lie around your apartment all day wishing for a million dollars and it will show up in your mailbox. There's more to manifestation than just simply wanting something. You need to put in hard work; you have to earn it. I didn't just make a silly wish to get my dream home; I sat for days on end in that house attending to thankless and commission-less open houses. I made life choices in line with that wish that would one day put me in the perfect position for it to come true, whether it was eventually making my own money moves as a real estate agent or meeting the man of my dreams who checked off all the boxes: kind, supportive, brilliant, and successful in his own right. I was also journaling, making vision boards, and working the steps of a gratitude practice (all things we'll talk about later in this chapter), which perfectly aligned my wavelengths with the Universe's.

Manifestation, or the practice of thinking big, diamond-studded aspirational thoughts with the goal of making them a reality, is like the perfect cocktail—it's just the right balance between choosing the right dream (as in, ballsy and BOLD) and being as specific as possible, with a generous pour of hustle and a twist of magic. And if you don't believe that's possible for you, then you may as well skip to the next chapter or, better yet, quit this book while you're ahead, because that kind of small, shitty attitude will only manifest small, shitty things. And I want nothing to do with that.

I do get, however, if you're feeling a bit skeptical—that's totally OK. But I didn't make this stuff up—it's even rooted in science. According to research conducted by Dr. Carol Dweck, a professor of psychology at Stanford University who's known for her work on mindset, believing you can do something makes it more likely that you'll be successful in doing it. She asserts that our beliefs about how what we can achieve and how we can succeed—what she calls our "growth mindset"—can actually affect whether we can make our desires come true. The main reason for this is that the more we truly, deeply, honestly know that we can achieve something, then we're willing to do the hard work to achieve it. That's a very different story than other flavors of manifestation where some people will tell you that belief alone is enough. Research also shows that what we hope to happen tends to be confirmed, or what's called a "self-fulfilling prophecy." Heard of it? It basically means that if you expect something to happen, whether it's good or bad, the outcome is likely to go that way. Call me crazy all you want—people a lot smarter than me have found it to be true in their studies. But enough talk—let's get down to it.

* * *

What most people don't know about me is that when you're in my corner and are someone I care about, I will be your biggest cheerleader and supporter. And I love giving advice—hence this book—plus, I'm really fucking good at it. It's the Libra in me; I'm the rock you can depend on and go to for guidance. That's why I love this chapter so much, because it's my number-one recommendation when people come to me wanting to know how I've built this incredible life. Hands-down it's manifestation. It wouldn't be right for it to be the first chapter in this book because of all the preparatory work and setting the mental stage that's required, but it's definitely the most important one. It's where you're really going to start seeing your dreams come true. Trust in the process, give it up to the Universe, and we're going to get you there.

There are a number of exercises that I love as part of my manifestation practice—journaling, vision boarding, visualization, giving gratitude, and taking action—and we'll break down what each of them is and what they entail in a minute. But first, you have to learn the basics behind the manifesting; you have to understand, deeply and without hesitation, what makes the magic work. Like I said before, now's not the time for limited thinking and doubt; that will only bring you more of the same in your life. This is the final stop before we dive in and summon all the riches that you deserve, so make your choice—are you in or are you out?

Each of the manifestation methods described in this chapter has three things in common: You have to be suuuper clear on what you want; you have to know why it means something to you; and you have to feel it so intensely in your bones that you can see, hear, taste, and feel it whenever you close your eyes. So now you see the method to my madness—I'm not just a crazy

bitch; there's a reason I had you spend every single chapter leading up to this getting to know yourself, seeing the outcomes that
you want, tasting the blood in the water like a motherfucking
shark. Think of this as your graduation from boot camp and
earning your fabulous scout badges. My little bitchy babies are
all grown up and making the lives they want and deserve! Now
get out there and make this mama proud.

Here's what you need to do first, and then apply it to whatever manifestation method you choose:

1. **Get crystal fucking clear.** I'm talking down to the last
Swarovski crystal on that baby pink dress you're wearing to the
Cannes premiere of your first feature film. The Universe can't
deliver on wishy-washy whining. Instead, guide the Universe
with solid direction and intention. I get that you might feel like
you've lost your mind coming up with these far-fetched dreams,
but you didn't always feel that way. Remember when you were
a kid—nothing was off the table when you were playing make-
believe. You didn't wish you were a mermaid and then go, "Oh,
but I guess that would never happen?" You'd be one downer of
a four-year-old if you did. No, you splashed around in that tub
with your purple iridescent tail, seashell bra, and Ariel hair,
knowing in your little heart that you made one fucking amazing
mermaid and that life was better with a little fantasy. Then you
learned apprehensions as an adult. You were told over and over
to not reach for your dreams but to reach for what was reasonable, what was expected—school, a job, a marriage, some kids.
But what if you kept wishing you were a mermaid? You might
not live under the sea, but don't you think your life could have
a little more sparkle? Your job now is to go back to that child's
mindset that believes anything is possible and then see it from

all angles—the same way a child would sit down to draw their superhero-princess-firefighter dreams. Because lucky for you, you can bring that magic back any time you want.

2. **Make it matter.** Yeah, yeah, yeah, more money, more things, more love, more passion. We all want it all. What makes the difference between manifestation and just another wish in the fountain is why it matters to *you*. What about this particular goal would make your life better? What would make it significant in your life in particular? Think about how exactly you'd use that money—would you pay off student debt? Would you see the world and use the experiences to launch your writing career? Would it be fuck-you money, showing anyone in your life who said you'd never amount to anything that they're a big fucking idiot? If you found the person of your dreams, what would that mean for your life? Would every day be a little more beautiful because you could share the things that make you happy with someone else? Or if you finally got that house or apartment you've been salivating over—how would that give you a leg up in life? Would it mean that you could throw parties for people you love in order to celebrate how much they matter to you? Would it make a better life for your family?

I want you to really dig in here. The Universe knows when you're manifesting something meaningful and special versus a goal that's shallow. I mean, you know I'm a Material Girl, but all the big, glossy things I've manifested into my life were so I could build an outside that matches the inside. And as we've discussed at length now, the more you live in your truth, the more giving, more generous, more loving you can be. Putting that kind of energy and intention out into the world sends positive wavelengths far and wide. So don't just think of it as making your own dreams come true; think of it as making the world a better place. If you're being honest about that, the Universe will answer.

I also want you to use this step of the process to really connect with whether your goal is the right fit for you. Is it truly what you want, or is it what someone else wants for you? Or what you think you *should* want? Will it make you feel happy and fulfilled? Things that you believe in and have positive associations with are more likely to be answered.

3. **Let's get visual.** There was an amazing study done on visualization and Olympic athletes and how picturing the act of something can affect actual results. For days and days, every single day, these elite runners would loop around the track for practice, doing the same circuit over and over again, round and round. Then the researchers took them to a lab and hooked them up to a brain-scanning technology and asked them to run the track in their minds as if they were doing it in real life. So they sat there and envisioned it, ready set go, the whole deal. They ran the track in their brains the way they'd done it thousands of times before. Next, they went back out to the track, still hooked up to the brain-scanner thingies, so they could actually run. And you know what? The scans showed that the brain could not tell the difference between when the athletes were running or just running the track in their minds. That's how powerful visualization is. It's the literal proof of setting your mind to something. And when that happens, it's putting a powerful plan into motion.

The more clearly you can see your new bag/car/job/partner/body/life in your mind's eye, the more of an immediate emotional connection you'll have with it, and the more intensely you'll be leading the manifestation charge from the very bottom of your soul. That kind of confidence and conviction is what screams to the Universe: Lay it on me, bitch!

This is why getting clear about your goals is the first step of the manifestation process. You can't visualize something in the most intimate detail if you don't know exactly what you want. By the time you start introducing your manifestation goals to your brain, they should be as fully formed as possible. Like I said, down to the last freckle on your dream man's shoulder, letterhead of your dream job position, cabinet pulls in your dream kitchen, and flecks of sand on your dream beach.

<u>MANIFESTATION METHOD 1:</u>
<u>JOURNALING</u>

When most people think of journaling, they think of slipping into their jammies, sipping on some wine, and spilling the day's events. Dear Journal, today I took a shower, had coffee, went to work, ordered takeout, texted with that cute guy I met last Saturday, and watched the entire first season of *FBoy Island*. Aw, so sweet. But also, boring! If this is you, then you're at a 5 right now, and we need you at a 10. This journal isn't just for what happened in your life, it's for what's *going to happen* in your life.

I've always kept a journal, but at one point I realized two things: I was spending most of my time either complaining about things that I didn't like (mostly the bitches at the office, lbh) or just parroting back the events of the day. I lived my life, wrote it down, done. But there was no *intention* behind it.

Nothing shifting the cycle or moving the needle. I was only calling in more of the same at best, or more negativity at worst.

So a few years ago, I started experimenting with jotting down what I did that day, and then sprinkling in some things that I wanted to happen alongside what was actually happening in my life. I'd just sandwich these teeny, tiny white lies between the truths so they blended in seamlessly. For example, take what I did to manifest a *Vogue* cover: I'd say something like "Today I went out for my usual macadamia matcha latte (true), then I met my stylist for a brainstorming sesh for some new looks for my upcoming Amalfi trip (true). I'm so excited to be taking baby Christian on his first trip to Europe! (Also true). Then OMG, I got a call to be on the cover of *Vogue!* I can't believe my dream has finally come true." (Teeny, tiny white lie). Sure enough, six months ago it happened. The cover of *Vogue*?! No one gets that; it's impossible. But it was a personal goal of mine that I lived out in my manifesting over and over.

Or maybe I'd say something like "I spent the morning cuddling with baby Christian before getting up to do an extra-sweaty yoga session with my trainer. I wrapped up just in time to get a call from my publisher, who was ringing to let me know that my book had officially hit the *New York Times* bestseller list. Then, I snuck in a couple of interviews before giving myself the afternoon to have a relaxing lunch with friends." See what I did there? Ever since I knew that my next goal was to be an author—scratch that, a *New York Times*-bestselling author—I'd work that into my daily entries.

Over time, this has a powerful effect on your brain and, eventually, your brand. It's creating these affirmations for your mind, which doesn't know the difference between what you're writing on paper and the reality that you're living. Eventually, the line begins to blur between what's real and what's not. Meanwhile, because your brain is completely on board with this new-and-improved version of you, you actually start living your life as though these things are real. That's the secret sauce to starting to invite incredible changes.

So I want you to dedicate at least five minutes a day to journaling. Buy yourself a journal that's pretty and special-feeling. Splurge on one that seriously feels like a treat to open and write in, one that sits on your nightstand and looks worthy of capturing your deepest, most urgent desires. This journal is a magic portal to creating the future of your dreams, and I'm not sure that janky notebook that you used for high school calc is going to offer the kind of pixie dust that we're looking for. Throw in a pen, too—the extra-nice kind with ink that's smooth as silk. Then treat this practice like it's sacred. Do it every. Single. Night. Or morning. Whatever. But you have to do it every day. In the beginning, it might feel strange to be writing about things that haven't really happened, but you'll be surprised how quickly it'll start to seem completely natural. Especially if you've chosen these aspirational elements wisely, they should seem like they're part of the life that you were born for. Because you were! Stick with this for at least twenty-one days, which is how long it takes to form a habit. After that, it'll feel like a necessary part of your day that's as essential as brushing your teeth or your ten-step skincare routine.

MANIFESTATION METHOD 2: VISION BOARDING

Like many of my manifestation practices, I didn't really know that this was even a thing or had a name when I started doing it. For me, I saw it as a way to make a sort of checklist, a collage of all the things I wanted to achieve, made all the more real because every day I could look at something concrete versus just the fantasies in my head. I had all these goals for what I wanted my life to look like, incredible places I wanted to go, fashion with all that extra drip—the works. So, as I would see the *exact* images of these things in magazines or online, I'd clip them out and tack them onto a board. There was the $40,000-a-night suite on the beach in Cabo, flying first-class on Lufthansa drinking champagne and eating chilled caviar, the black Rolls Royce that I really wanted, even the Daytona Rolex that I was lusting after. I got really, really specific. Then I tucked it away in my closet one day—mainly because, again, I had no idea that I was sending up some kind of bat signal to the Universe—and didn't really think about it until two or three years later. I unearthed it one day, took that baby out, and I shit you not, every single thing had come true. At the time I made the board, each of these things was completely unachievable, laughable even. My husband drove that *exact* same car. I had *that* Rolex. I had even been on that *exact* vacation—but with the wrong guy, unfortunately. Because I hadn't been specific enough!

Again, I don't credit some kind of bogus hocus-pocus for this. I truly believe it's because I'd gotten so insanely specific that my brain started sending my body some kind of directions, like I'd actually changed my programming. Then I went out and made that shit happen. It's like if *Practical Magic* and *Working Girl* had a baby—a little enchantment mixed with sheer scrappiness and force of will.

Over time, I tweaked my process to combine vision boarding with journaling since they're a tag-team manifestation power couple. Even though I'm such a visual person, I find writing things down to be really powerful, too. So I would make a board but also write things in with a Sharpie, like "I'm so thankful my husband is so amazing. He's so funny, he's so loyal, he's so this, he's so that, he looks like that." Or "I'm so grateful for this house that I love. It's four bedrooms, five bathrooms, and right on the beach." Even if it's just a few little sentences that declare what you're looking for, it helps leave nothing open to interpretation. Because as we know, the Universe is a very literal creature, and she can be a bit of a tricky bitch.

Another version that I like to play with, too, is a vision board that incorporates my schedule and actual plans that are in the works. I use a tri-fold poster board and label each section with an upcoming month (June, July, August, for example). Then I'll write down the big things I have going on that month, along with a list of goals for each one. So, for example, I'll pencil in my cover shoot for *Grazia* magazine, a timeline for a makeup campaign that's coming out, and a photo shoot for my book cover. All of these things are real and happening, so my brain is already churning out the planning. I harness that momentum to aim a little higher and sprinkle in some things on my wish list. For example, I might pencil in "interview creative directors for clothing line," "brainstorming meeting for my own TV show," or "research trip to Morocco." Some are feasible while others are shooting for the stars. But you write it all down. And if something doesn't happen in that particular month, then just roll it over into the next month. It's an amazing way to break up some loftier goals into more achievable segments and keep you on track to get exactly where you want to go. Meanwhile, your brain is getting used to seeing the goals that you have achieved and checked off next to goals that you're still working for because, as we know by now, your brain is a superpowered machine that can see past, present, and future all at the same time.

Or, if you're looking to get super focused on a specific area of your life, you can make a "mini" board for just that manifestation. A great example of this is when I used a mini board to call in money. When I first started in real estate, I received a check for $8,000 on some lease I did. I wrote over that amount with a Sharpie so it became a new check to Christine Quinn for $100,000 from the Oppenheim Group—just for visualization purposes. I put the check on a shelf in my closet and looked at it every single day. Do I realize how ridiculous this sounds? Yes. A check for $100,000? That was an insane amount of money for a baby agent; hell, it's an insane amount of money now. But as you know, I dream big. And I kept that check right in my line of sight while working hard at my job. After about a year, when I finally got my first listing, I sold that house and a few weeks later got a check from the Oppenheim Group. For $83,000. Close enough, right? I come across that check every so often and just cry—tears of happiness, tears of joy, tears of knowing that for once in my life I am finally the one in control.

There's no wrong way to make a vision board; do it the way that feels most natural to you. If you're just starting out, go old-school with a poster board, a glue stick, and some magazine cutouts. Over time, hone your style and what feels most powerful.

Before getting started, take a minute to get really clear on what you want to bring into your life. Think about all the biggies: travel, life, home, and career. Next, start looking for images—in magazines, online, and so on. Google can be your best friend. But again, you need to be *specific* with your overall vision. When I added a picture of a bride and groom to my board, I pasted my head on the bride's body—ain't no other bitch gonna catch my man! Don't just settle for some generic version of your life; that totally defeats the purpose.

Regardless of how you create your board, make sure you're consistently looking at your masterpiece. Just as with journaling, the more you do this and the more you convince yourself that you're gazing at your future in the magic ball, the more likely it is that all of your dreams will come true.

MANIFESTATION METHOD 3: VISUALIZATION

I learned the following exercise years ago and I think it's a great starting point if you're new to manifestation. It's also a good one to use if you have a hard time sitting still, like I do, since it's shorter than a meditation and involves active imagining instead of having to clear your mind. Um, yeah, never been too good at that—this girl needs her mental checklists. Visualization, or picturing your goals as if you're watching them happen in real life, is similar to journaling or vision boarding in that you're—not to sound like a broken record here—getting specific, making it meaningful, and then giving your goals the kind of visuals that align your brain and body. I love using visualization when I'm just waking up and am still lying in bed, or just before I fall asleep. Since I'm already relaxed and lying down, all I need to do is close my eyes and get into the manifesting zone. I'd reach for this technique a lot when I was transitioning out of my acting career (some actors even refer to this as method acting) but still wanted to find a way to be on TV, and I definitely used it to tune in when manifesting my *Vogue* cover. I'd picture myself on the cover itself, writing about it on social media, even getting a copy in the mail and displaying it on the mirror in my styling room. Try this exercise with your own dreams and desires—you'll see what a jolt your manifesting gets once you've completely gotten into your body and on the Universe-calling wavelength.

Start by lying down in a comfortable spot—your bed, the terrace of your Italian villa, the deck of your yacht, the usual. You're going to scan your entire body, checking in with all your big bits—head, belly, arms, hands, legs, feet—just enough to bring your attention there. There's no wrong way to do this, so if you're feeling restless from head toe, that's okay. This will get easier the more you do it. Be patient with yourself.

The idea is to take you out of your head and into your body just long enough to feel really grounded, which is what's going to make your mind super sharp. You can make this part of the process as long as you want, too, and go through dozens of body parts, or you if you're tight on time and want to make sure you sneak this into your day, just hit the biggies:

First, bring your attention to the top of your head. What does it feel like right now? Noisy? Quiet? Calm? Anxious? No judgment—just notice.

Then move down to the space between your eyebrows. Is it tense? Relaxed? Need a shot of Botox? Jk.

Now feel your eyes. Are they rolling around behind your eyelids? Shifting left? right? Are they heavy and still in the sockets?

Feel your breath. Is your stomach rising and falling? Or are you breathing more into your chest? Are your breaths quick and shallow, or long and deep?

Now, focus on your fingers. Are they moving? Still? Where are they resting on your body?

How do your legs feel? Are they heavy? Antsy?

What about your feet?

Once you're done with this body scan, it's time to start tuning into your desires and whatever it is you want to manifest. If you're still feeling restless, a trick I like to use to get out of my head is to imagine myself walking up a long hallway of stairs. Whatever those stairs look like is up to you. Visualize yourself walking up one hundred stairs and count each step in your mind as you do it. This will help settle down your mind from the day and inhibit useless thoughts or anxiety-inducing information from popping into your head. Continue counting your steps until you reach the top at the hundredth step. Then that is when the visualization begins. Whatever you do, *don't* start manifesting until you have reached the hundredth step and have cleared your head. Then it's time to let your mind take it away. Think about it like a movie that you're playing for yourself in your mind. Watch yourself actually experiencing the things that you want—boarding that plane, finding your seat, flying over the mountains as you descend down to that swanky ski resort. See the clothes you're unpacking from your suitcase: the creamy cashmere sweaters, Chanel ski boots, and après ski fashion. Or maybe it's walking into the first day of your new job, the view from your office, the sound of your assistant answering your phone.

Alternatively, you could use this more simple visualization technique that's helpful when you find yourself in a negative space and need to shake yourself out of it. Let's say you want to leave a job, or a relationship, or any other stuck-in-a-rut situation. You can even use this technique if you just want to get rid of a negative thought that's taken up space in your head, like self-doubt, bad vibes about a person, or anxiety about an upcoming event. Here's what you'll do:

I want you to revisit those stairs and visualize a white staircase—any kind will do. Super modern, cottage chic, whatever—just make it stairs and make them white. Now visualize yourself walking down that staircase toward a door with a big, red EXIT sign above it. As you watch yourself walking down that white staircase, counting each stair for focus, tell yourself, "I'm going to walk down these stairs, and when I walk out of that door, I'm no longer going to be worried about that project/man/job/situation." Really own that statement and believe it to be true. Then, when you've quieted all the voices, those bright, white stairs will fade to black. And as you hear the sound of the door slamming behind you, imagine that you're closing the door on your anxieties and locking it tight. Leave all that shit behind and don't turn back. This is particularly important because remember, the Universe can't hold up its end of the bargain if you're gunking up your messaging with hang-ups, holdbacks, grudges, and other negative thinking.

MANIFESTATION METHOD 4: BRING THE ACTION

I like to think of this as the extra credit, the secret sauce. It's what, I believe, has taken all of my manifestation practices over the edge from fantasy into the reality. While, yes, getting your brain on board with your goals is a super-important element of manifestation, so is putting that shit into high gear. And the way I like to do that is through dedicated action. Your actions, every single day, need to replicate what you want. For example, after this book got picked up by my publisher, I asked my sister—who helps me out with these things—to send flowers thanking them for taking a chance on me and my message. She asked me what I wanted the card to say, so I told her, "I'm so excited for this journey and look forward to this *New York Times* bestseller!" She was a little confused, but I needed it to be in writing. I'm always doing things like that and don't care if I look fucking crazy. After that, I made my own mockup of my book's cover and I put "*New York Times* bestseller" across the stop. I put that image as the wallpaper on my phone, and every time I walked by an airport bookstore, I'd stop for a minute so I could imagine my book right there on the New Releases shelf. Like anything in life, if you want something to happen, you have to get out there and make it work.

I like to think that taking action toward what you're manifesting is also like shaking something loose in the Universe. It's kind of like getting off the track you're on—the well-worn path that would lead you directly to more of the same—and then challenging the Universe to rewrite your story as it tries to keep up with where you're walking. Maybe my story didn't originally have me rocking a President Rolex with a diamond bezel, but I got the attention of the cosmic writer's room by always having a picture from the catalog handy so the image was seared into my brain and going to try it on in the store (multiple times). I combined that with putting in the extra hustle at work, challenging myself to make more connections and pick up a few extra clients, all with my eye on the blinged-out prize. I put the wheels in motion, and the Universe packaged it all up into a beautiful emerald green leather box.

MANIFESTATION METHOD 5: START A GRATITUDE PRACTICE

This isn't technically about manifestation, but it's something that I regularly practice, and I highly recommend that you do, too, because it's another powerful way to shape your life and everything in it. It's not just a powerful way of dealing with the shit that life regularly throws at us—difficulties, anxiety, frustration, basic bitches at the office (or is that just me?)—but you can also think of it as a way of making your beacon to the Universe shine a little brighter. I mean, if your head isn't all mucked up with stress or anger, it's going to connect much more strongly with your manifesting frequencies. Also, when you take a moment to appreciate the abundance that you already have in your life, you're not just showing up to the Universe empty-handed, whining about all the things that you don't have. If there's one thing that Divine Intervention doesn't vibe with, it's an attitude of lack. It doesn't want to hear how it's let you down—because it hasn't—it wants to hear about all the magic that you're creating and will continue to create with a little cosmic assist. And the best way to do that is with gratitude.

It's really that simple: Be grateful. Say thank you. It's not bullshit. It's impossible to get caught up in the bad vibes if you're simultaneously feeling #blessed. For example, not so long ago I had this horrible scene where I was fighting with one of the girls. I mean I wasn't in a fight; she came at me. She was all up in my face saying *fuck you* this and *fuck you* that. The old me would have Gone. Off. Like, let me tell you what a bitch you are, you fucking bitch. But instead, I was able to stay totally calm. All I could think in my mind was *I actually feel bad for you because I have a baby and a husband at home who I really want to spend time with*. Even in the thick of all that drama, I could reach for all the gratitude. I had way too much to be happy about to let any bullshit get in the way. Then the entire way home, instead of focusing on that psycho bitch, I was like *It's not her fault that she's divorced and has a Rolodex of failures when I have all these things to be grateful for—I'm grateful for my husband; I'm grateful for my baby; I'm grateful I get to go home to them.* Know what I mean?

I work a gratitude practice two ways. First, I like to call in gratitude all the time, making sure that the tank is always filled. That way, if I find myself surrounded by negativity (um, have you seen my show?) or being attacked by negative people (same question), I'm locked and loaded with a high-vibe frequency. I do this by taking a moment whenever I can—when I'm driving, when I'm practicing yoga, when I'm getting my hair and makeup done in my glam room, or when I'm sipping a pint of draft Guinness at the end of a long day. (Surprise! It's not all Dom for this girl.) It doesn't have to take a long time; it just has to take up meaningful space in your brain for a moment or two. I run through the list—baby, man, house, job—and in just a minute I'm buzzing with gratitude for what I have and excitement for what can come in the future.

The other way I work in more gratitude is by using it to create a shift in my brain if I find myself having negative thoughts. Even when I'm surrounding myself with positivity and a sunny attitude, I can still get sucked into the petty bullshit, anxious thoughts, or other downer cycles. That's when I reach for the remote and just change the channel. I think about things that make me happy (baby Christian, awww), read a book I'm loving (anything by my girl Lauren Weisberger), or watch a feel-good movie (*The Devil Wears Prada*—I'm telling you, that Lauren can do no wrong). Go for anything that gives you instant gratification, whether that's playing video games, baking cookies, or knitting a fucking blanket. Then, when your mind is no longer fixated on whatever shitty situation has been living rent-free in your brain, start filling it with new, positive thoughts. Because I have so much practice training my brain to not get caught in that glitch, I can luckily snap out of it pretty easily. Over time, you'll see how seamlessly you can switch from the negative to the positive, too.

CHAPTER 8

THE SHAME SHAM

Women shaming women is not a mind-blowingly new concept. Most women do it without even noticing it, some do it as a hobby, and others do it like it's an Olympic fucking sport. But here's the deal: It's hard enough being a woman in a mansplaining, appearance-obsessed world, so I say we all agree to put an end to the bullshame once and for all. And maybe, just maybe, we can lift each other up with kindness and compassion instead—starting with ourselves.

Don't worry; I'm not getting all kumbaya on you (patchouli def doesn't go with this Prada), but if you're going to reach your full Boss Bitch potential, then that little voice in your head that automatically criticizes other women has got to go. Because, if we're really being honest with each other and ourselves, that little voice comes from something you probably just don't like about yourself. And we're not about that life. Instead, if you want to have a shot at leveling up, you need to lean into your biggest, baddest, most authentic self.

And you know what that doesn't include? Getting up in other people's business.

Take it from me, I've experienced every form of shaming that exists: slut shaming, body shaming, plastic surgery shaming, bitch shaming. It's not easy out there for a larger-than-life Boss B who knows her mind, loves her body, and isn't afraid to own when she's had a little work done to make the exterior match the fabulous interior. I'm a big-time believer that the way you want to put yourself out into the world is exactly the way it should be and that no one else has a say in that. So, if you're out there yucking someone else's yums, you have to ask yourself why. What feelings come up for you? Are you angry? Jealous? I know it can seem like a cop-out to say, "You're just jealous," but so many of us women feel like we're not allowed to really let our light shine, so when we see someone else who does and is out there fucking owning it, it can be a little #triggering. That's why I wanted to devote a chapter to really looking at what's keeping you back from being the biggest, brightest bitch out there. Because this is officially your permission to do that, no matter what that looks like for you. And that starts with shutting the fuck up about other women, turning that energy inward, and figuring out how you want to live your own most authentic life.

WE HAVE TO DO BETTER: HERE IS HOW WE START

In order to put an end to the shame game, you need to do three things:

1. **Make peace with the girl in the mirror.**

2. **Build other women up.**

3. **Call out the haters.**

You know I can be a little naughty when it comes to being in it for the drama, but I *never* do it at the expense of bringing someone else down for bringing them down's sake. It's always rooted in truth. You know how they say "Justice is blind"? She most definitely is *not*—she's an eagle-eyed bitch who knows petty bullshit when she sees it and isn't afraid to call it out. Just look at her standing there with her Halston-inspired gown and fabulous scales—she most definitely knows what's up. But she's not about tearing down a bitch just to make herself feel better. No, she's about holding up the things that matter: fairness, accuracy, and righteousness. How can we be more like Lady J? Let's start with making a little love to ourselves.

<u>STEP 1: MAKE PEACE WITH THE GIRL IN THE MIRROR</u>

I didn't always feel beautiful. Maybe it was because I was gawky and awkward from the time I hit puberty, or maybe it was because people treated me like shit because I didn't look like the popular girls at school. It made me go to such a negative place, resenting other girls for being prettier or for boys liking them—even though they were totally basic. Instead of seeing my own great qualities and feeling secure enough to not need to bash anyone else to make myself feeling better, I was coming from such a negative place. But I realized that the more I liked myself, the less I needed to come after anyone else.

To look in the mirror and love what you see is a skill that not everyone is born with. But I am living proof that you can get to a place where that girl staring back at you is your ride or die. The first step that I took was figuring out what I wanted to see in the mirror. I wanted to figure out a way for my outside to reflect my inside. This went way deeper than the clothes I wore; this was about being comfortable in my own skin. At the time, I was watching a ton of old movies, especially *Gentleman Prefer Blondes*. I watched that damn movie over and over and over again, any chance I got. When other kids were watching MTV and doing their best Avril Lavigne impressions, I was home with Marilyn Monroe and Jane Russell, soaking up their every move. I was especially smitten with Marilyn (could you have guessed?) and the way she did everything with so much confidence—spoke, moved, even just stood still. I loved her curvy body and the way she used it to project confidence. I did the same thing with videos of Dolly Parton, watching her performances in concerts and movies like *9 to 5* and *Steel Magnolias*. I was in awe of not just her voice and her amazing tits, but the way she commanded an audience. She and Marilyn used the assets they had, and it made them powerful.

I started taking a page from the Fake It 'til You Make It playbook. I imagined myself speaking and moving like them, as though I were the one in the movies. When I watched them, I saw myself. I mimicked the way they'd swish their hips, Dolly's power poses, and Marilyn's girly laugh. As they say, imitation is the sincerest form of flattery, so this was definitely me worshipping at the altar. But I wasn't Single White Female-ing them, I was borrowing their signature traits to help project things about myself that I hadn't been able to do before. When I watched them, I not only saw things that I admired, I saw parts of me that I'd never been able to express. And over time, I added my own flair to make it mine. For example, instead of copying Marilyn's classic bob, I wanted a long, Barbie-like mane. Instead of Dolly's Appalachia-chic look, I wanted full-on glam. But I give full credit to them for helping me develop my own traits, mannerisms, vibe, and attitude that eventually became Christine the Brand.

Another great exercise for a self-esteem boost is to write yourself love notes. No, I didn't just have a cheesed-out stroke. I think a lot of us take time to be grateful for things that happen to us, but we don't stop to give ourselves the love we deserve, whether it's hyping ourselves up, writing love letters to ourselves, or saying, "Fuck it; I'm my biggest fan." I'm a true believer in setting daily mantras—they're a powerful way of stating your truth and then fully embodying that truth. In this case, make your mantras centered around telling yourself how amazing you are. "You are so beautiful," "No one else can match your creativity," "Your curves are what make you sexy," "You're the smartest bitch I know." You get the gist. You could also do the same thing with journaling, having a check-in every morning or evening to set this new intention until it feels second nature. If you need to fake it, then fake it. Tell yourself how amazing you are and how gorgeous you are and how much you love yourself until something clicks and you believe every single word that you're saying.

STEP 2: BUILD OTHER WOMEN UP

We live in an image-obsessed society, and while complimenting another woman on her shoes or her nails is great, we need to dig a little deeper. It's time to give props where props are due to the women in our lives who we truly, deeply admire for reasons beyond how they slay an outfit. Think about how you feel when you're in full-on Boss Bitch mode—like you could conquer the world Oprah-style, right? Now think about what gets you into that zone—you're feeling yourself, right? So imagine what your city, state, country, fuck, *world* would be like if we built a Boss Bitch army full of women who are that driven. My guess is that we could solve some of our biggest issues with enough time to break for lunch and a deep tissue.

So how can we harness the power of the Boss B? It starts with paying it forward. It's time to build each other up and get that momentum going. I want you to identify three women in your life who you admire and really think about why. Then, you're going to make their day by sharing those reasons with them. Go beyond their best physical features, or what they wear. Who are the women in your life who you want to stand up and applaud? What is it about them that makes you feel that way? What traits do they have that are unique to them? I'll start with three well-known women who I've been lucky enough to meet.

MINDY KALING

I met Mindy in a really funny way. I was waiting to walk into a scene on *Selling Sunset* (they always hold me for the drama of a grand entrance . . . are you surprised?). And this woman comes up to me with a mask on and she's screaming behind the mask, "Oh my God, Christine! Christine!" I thought she was a cute fangirl at first, but then she came closer, took off her mask, and it was Mindy fucking Kaling. I couldn't believe it.

Then she says to me, "I'm obsessed with you. I love everything about you; I'm your biggest stalker. You have no idea.
Congrats on the baby and the book, I'm so excited for you. I literally love you. Team Christine."

How's that for women lifting up other women?

"Girl, I love *you*!" I told her. "I'm actually *your* biggest stalker!"
But there's more. Mindy, here's why I admire you:

It started, as I'm sure it did for many of your fans, with *The
Office*, which I used to watch on repeat. I've seen every single
episode, largely because of you. You have this dry humor while
being so sweet, relatable, and likeable. It was a rare combination for a woman on TV back then, in the pre-Netflix era! You
were self-aware before self-awareness was even a thing. You
were ahead of your time, and you've gone on to achieve so much
in Hollywood, like creating *The Sex Lives of College Girls*. (Binged,
obsessed). The pleasure of our meeting was all mine.

KHLOÉ KARDASHIAN

I've been a fan of the Kardashians for years, so you can imagine
my surprise and total delight when Khloé and I started DMing
each other on Instagram. We have a mutual friend who first
put us in touch, and we completely hit it off. Khloé had a lot of
really sweet advice for me about becoming a mom. In fact, she
was one of the first people I told about my pregnancy.

As a fan of your show, Khloé, I was drawn to you from the
start. It was obvious to me that you are a natural-born star. You
were just so yourself, so genuine, so hilarious. You were unapologetically yourself on that show, and to me, there is simply nothing
better. Now, between your company, Good American—bringing

fashion to EVERY body—and being a mom, you're killing the game. I'm proud of you.

SIMONE BILES

I was lucky enough to get a DM from the GOAT gymnast back when I got engaged to Christian: "You're my favorite person, literally," she wrote. "I love you. I want to be you when I grow up." I meannn!

We've exchanged lots of messages since then, and I absolutely love that she's decorated her leotards with a rhinestone goat. Gotta love that bling, girl! It's sadly all too rare for female athletes to own their power the way Simone does. That just comes down to confidence. She doesn't fit the mold of what people want gymnasts to be (ahem, quiet and amenable little girls). I love when people do fuck shit up and don't follow the rules, so I obviously stan Simone.

Simone, I love everything that you do. On top of being extremely talented, I love your attitude and your flair. You exude confidence. Someone could perform the exact same skills as you in gymnastics, but it wouldn't be the way you do them. There's something visual, and visceral, about your inner confidence and the way you seize your greatness. And on top of all your accomplishments, the fact that you prioritized your mental health and pulled out of the Olympic Team All-Around when you weren't in the right headspace to compete set an amazing, valuable, potentially lifesaving example to people everywhere. It's easy to look at successful women and assume they don't have struggles and difficulties, but we all do. Chipping away at the stigma about mental health is so important, and you did that like the GOAT that you are. Thank you for being you.

This book wouldn't be complete without me also giving some love to other amazing women in my life who inspire me and lift me up, such as Chrissy Teigen, Miranda Kerr, Lisa Rinna, Tyra Banks, and Leyla Milani-Khoshbin.

STEP 3: CALL OUT THE HATERS

Let's be real—most shaming happens online. The majority of Internet trolls don't have the balls to take their criticism and contempt for other women from the keyboard to the real world. It's easy to spew hate from the safety of your laptop; it's a lot harder to do it face-to-face. Lucky for you, calling out the woman-shamers is also a lot easier to do online. If you're scrolling on your phone anyway, why not put that time to good use? When you see someone harassing another woman, call them out. You can do it in your own words, or you can borrow mine. Jot this down, or copy and paste it:

> *Hey there! I see you took the time to share your thoughts about [enter woman's name]. While I respect that you have an opinion, have you stopped to consider that if you used your time in a positive way instead that the world would be a nicer place to live in? And maybe people would be nicer to you in return? Sending you love!*

See, you gotta kill 'em with kindness. Or if it's a woman tearing another woman down, consider going with this:

Hi! It's so great that we have this amazing platform where we can all share our ideas, but what if women stopped acting like enemies and started behaving like we're all on the same team? What if instead of dragging each other down we tried lifting each other up? Pass it on.

I mean, what if we all made this our pet project? We could completely change what it's like to share things online. Instead of instantly worrying whether someone's going to come at us for every little thing—being too slutty, too strong, too loud, too outspoken, too strange—we could instead completely unleash knowing that we'd have this incredible community there to support us. Not to mention the fact that all these people who had essentially made a career out of tearing people down online, spending hours looking for the perfect mark, thinking of the perfect nasty comment, and being so proud of their sad little selves would now be totally out of business. Imagine what they could now do with all that newfound free time!

SHUT DOWN THE BODY SHAMING

I can't even believe we still have to talk about this—it's 20 fucking 21. Do we really need yet another lesson about how every body is beautiful exactly the way God or Dr. Godman made it? We'll get to nips and tucks in a minute, but first, let's end this nonsense once and for all: No matter what someone's body looks like, what size they are, or the clothes they choose to wear to show that body off—or hide it, if that's their preference or according to their beliefs—it is, clap along with me now: None. Of. Your. Fucking. Business. Don't go assuming that because someone looks a certain way that you know everything about them. Do you know how many women have called me anorexic? I was born a literal pole. I have a hard time putting on weight no matter what I do. I'm not saying that as a humble brag. Do you know how badly I wanted to be a Marilyn size 10? Her hips, her ass, her boobs— I wanted them all and felt like less of a woman because the only curvy thing on my body was my head. So I know firsthand about how when it comes to our looks, the grass is always greener on the other side. That's just human nature. But that doesn't mean you should go throwing manure over the fence!

My hat is off to women like Ashley Graham, Lizzo, and Bebe Rexha, who live in bodies that don't fit the stereotypical Hollywood mold. I love that, despite the fact that for so long we've been told women need to look a certain way in order to be beautiful, they own who they are and how they look with the hope that more women will accept themselves at any size. Falling outside of the "norm" when it comes to beauty standards doesn't make someone less gorgeous—it means that how we define it is just too limited. Open your minds, people!

Unfortunately, a lot of folks are still living under a rock when it comes to getting the memo that their shame-train ride has ended. So I encourage every single person reading this chapter to call them out and bring them over to the bright side. My guess is that almost every single hater who is taking the time to comment on someone else's body has a lot of house-keeping they need to do with themselves. Think about that for yourself, too. Any time you're tempted to call someone fat, or tell them that they can't wear a certain kind of clothing because of the size of their body, or tell someone to go eat a sandwich because they're too skinny, take a look at yourself first. How do you feel about yourself? If the answer is "not so great," then really take this section to heart. YOU ARE BEAUTIFUL! Exactly the way you are! All of us are! Cellulite, jiggly arms, soft bellies, big boobs, little boobs, lanky legs, short and stumpy legs—whatever. It's all amazing because it's what you do with it that counts. I'm willing to bet that the more confidence you have in yourself and the more you can look in a mirror and feel the love, the less inclined you'll be to take out your frustration on someone else. Remember, we're all in this together now and we're here for you!

PLASTIC FANTASTIC

While we're on the topic of getting all up in other people's business, I want to take a minute to put an end to shaming a woman for wanting to change what she looks like. We don't drag a woman for wanting to change the color of her hair, her eyes, or her nails, so why do we get all hot and bothered when it's her lips, tits, ass, brows, chin, calves, or whatever the fuck else? The way I see it, cosmetic surgery or injectables like filler and Botox are just one more way for women to look as good on the outside as they feel on the inside.

I remember back when I was in my Marilyn and Dolly days trying to see in the mirror what I was seeing on-screen, there was a disconnect. There was something about what was reflected back looking so different from how I felt in my brain that always nagged at me. So when I was twenty-one, I got my boobs done. It wasn't because I was comparing myself to other people; it was because I knew it would make me feel so much more confident and sexy. So I went out, worked super hard, and saved up the $7,000 to have the procedure done. It was something I did for myself and myself only. I mean, if I wanted to do it for a man, I would have at least had a man pay for it!

Then I started playing around with lip filler because I wanted big lips to fit my enormous mouth—and I don't just mean what comes out of it. After that came Botox, at first preventively and then as maintenance. I didn't do this because I hated myself. The total opposite! I did it because I *loved* myself, and I wanted my outside to reflect the gorgeous inside that I was so proud of. And I totally own that. The same way #bodypositivity has given women the freedom to embrace themselves in all shapes and sizes, I was applying that same adoration to myself, once I'd gotten to a place that finally looked and felt like the truest version of me. Believe me, there is no shame in this game.

In fact, I think people should be talking more about the work they've had done or want to get done. I remember when *Selling Sunset* first came out, there were all these articles about each of us women and all the cosmetic surgery that the "experts" were speculating we'd had done. I think that's so dangerous because it makes people feel like it's supposed to be a secret. No! Owning who we are includes the choices that we make to feel beautiful. Think about the alternative—all these fake-ass bitches on Instagram pretending to be perfect. That's even more damaging! No filter, my ass! No one is perfect—fuck, even after four hours of glam I used to Photoshop the shit out of my photos. Everyone does! Did any of these things change who I am? No. Does it enhance me? Yes. I do feel better. So let's all stop pretending to be born like this. I made these choices, and anyone else can, too. Which brings me to:

YOU DO YOU

My family and I were traveling after I wrapped the most recent season of the show, and an interesting subject came up between me and Christian. I was getting ready to go out to the beach, so I was putting on a little makeup—just a bit of concealer and some mascara. Then I decided to blow-dry my hair, too. Christian watched me do it.

"Why do you care what people think about the way you look?" he asked me, looking visibly perplexed.

"You don't understand," I told him. "This isn't about other people. It's about me. If I think I look like shit on the outside, then I'm going to feel like shit on the inside. Putting on mascara and drying my hair makes me feel good."

It all comes down to you do you, doesn't it? I know there are women who wouldn't think twice about not wearing makeup when going to the beach with their families. They would own a no-makeup, natural look, and I think that's awesome. But there are also tons of women who need to do a little of this and a little of that to feel good about themselves. Like anything else, we are all different in the way that we feel comfortable presenting ourselves to the world.

I simply cannot stress this enough: You do you. And that bitch over there? She's doing the same. You might look different from one another in the process, but that's what makes the world go 'round.

End the shame, even in little ways. If we all do our part, maybe we can be on the same team together after all.

CHAPTER 9

MILF MONEY

I always thought I'd seen it all when it came to woman-on-woman shaming, but it was never as intense as it was after I got pregnant with my son, birthed him, and started the hardest job of my life—raising him. And this might come as a shock, but I did it all without listening to a single word of input from all the people out there who feel like it's their job to critique, criticize, troll, diss, and harass their way into my life, especially when it comes to my kid.

This isn't the newest concept, but having a baby is utterly life changing. There is no time that a woman needs support more, and yet, it ends up being a time when everyone and literally their mother feels like it's open season on every last one of your decisions. Whether it's how you get pregnant—or decided not to!—carry your baby, birth your baby, and go back to living your life afterward, I want you to know that it is no one's fucking business. Full stop. I don't care if it's your best friend or your mom—hell, even your doctor needs to know when to stay in her lane when it comes to certain parenting decisions. This is all to say that when it comes to making money moves as a mom, it's your show and you get to call all the shots.

I experienced drive-by mom bashing at every single step of becoming a mom. When I was about six months along, I decided to announce my pregnancy in a People.com article. Almost immediately after the post went live, the criticism began:

"She's not six months pregnant!"

"Look at the size of her bump!"

"She's lying."

At first, I brushed it off. It was definitely weird how obsessed with my body people had gotten, and I didn't really understand why someone's thoughts would be so negative when they could just be happy for me. But I wasn't going to spend too much energy getting down about it. I mean, I never naturally had a butt or boobs, and I've always been skinny, so it made sense to me that my bump would be more Mini Cooper than Range Rover.

But nothing could have prepared me for the criticism that kept coming, getting more harsh and more intense with each passing day. The messages from total strangers were now flooding in:

"I can't believe you'd bring a child into this world."

"I hope your baby dies."

Isn't the Internet special?

In less dramatic—but equally puzzling—fashion, I noticed that being pregnant meant that perfect strangers felt entitled to advise me on how to take care of myself and my unborn child. When I started showing, that opened the door to the in-person commentary:

"Oh no, no, no, no—you can't do that if you're pregnant." I heard that over and over from people, and I know that countless other pregnant women do, too. From your caffeine intake to your activity level, if you're visibly pregnant, the world thinks they have the right to chime in. The Internet freaked out over my exercise regimen, which—c'mon people!—was nothing but yoga and Pilates, and which I'd been practicing well before I got pregnant. And if someone was going to be concerned about the safety of, say, inversions during my pregnancy, don't you think it would be me?? Of *course* I consulted the experts in my life who could advise me on how to move my body responsibly, and they all gave me the green light to continue doing the things that made me feel good. But to hear it from the comments on photos of me on the mat or the reformer, you'd think that someone needed to call Child Protective Services because I couldn't make those decisions for myself. And then there was the time when I was about eight months pregnant and a TV show that I was contracted to host abruptly canceled my appearance. My publicist inquired about the reason, and a producer said, "Oh, we thought she wouldn't want to do it anymore." Another show almost didn't invite me for the same reason. What is it about carrying a child that makes people believe that suddenly you can't think for yourself?? I know I'm about to become a mom to a human being and all, but thanks so much for making up my sad little mind for me. Jesus Christ.

Then there were people flipping out over what I wore. I mean, in my normal life I get a lot of slut-shaming because I'm all about that tits-out, legs-out life. And to that I say, "Thank you so much for noticing!" But during pregnancy? The naysayers were next-level downers. When I was pregnant, I was my usual sexy self—because I'm a true believer that nothing about you has to change just because you're a mom, personal style included. When I posed for *Playboy* at eight months pregnant, that's when people really started piling on. Apparently no one got the Demi

Moore *Vanity Fair* fabulousness memo because there were comments like:

"This is disgusting. Is *Playboy* really that desperate?"

"This is gross. No one wants to see this."

Gross? A woman's gorgeous, glowing pregnant body in all its amazing glory? Go back to the dark ages that you came from.

And don't even get me started on what came after baby Christian was born. Everyone and their mother had an opinion about how I should be living my postpartum life. I always knew that I wanted to get back to work pretty quickly after giving birth. That's just me. I love to work, and I don't believe that that has to change when you become a mom. I knew that I could balance giving Christian the care and love and attention he needed while also getting back to my favorite hustle. The producers of *Selling Sunset* made a comment while I was still pregnant along the lines of "You'll have a maternity leave." I told them that I would be the one deciding how much time I needed, not them. I wanted to be able to heal, and I'd be back as soon as I was physically ready. Instead of supporting me and my decision, they looked at me like I had two heads. And when I did return to filming—earlier than I was even ready to because of pressures from production, I might add—they only wanted me to do scenes if I was with my baby, including to the office. Clearly I love to show off my son, but I don't appreciate being put in the "mom box."

The show's producers weren't the only ones who couldn't keep their mouths shut. Cue the onslaught of commenters online:

"It's only been THREE weeks!"

"Who's taking care of your baby?" Um, none of your business?

"How are you doing this? You need to give yourself rest." Thanks for the "concern," but my body healed quickly. Did you want to schedule a conference call with my doctor?

"You're back to posting pictures of yourself? Where are the photos of the baby?" That's actually a funny one, because for every faux-panicked "Where's the baby?!" comment, there's someone else telling me they don't want to see baby pictures on my social media at all.

Some people might say that there's just no winning when it comes to being a mom and feeling like your decisions can't please everyone. But here's the thing: There is a way to win, and that starts with *not* pleasing everyone. I know that can come as a jolt to the system because we've been raised to be "nice girls" whose job it is to make everyone (but themselves) happy. And I know there's a lot of noise you have to ignore. But the upside is that you get to do you with absolutely no apologies, shame, or second-guessing necessary. There's no handbook for starting a family, and it looks different for everyone, so why not embrace what it is that you want and leave the rest alone. As Amy Poehler so geniously puts it in her book *Yes Please* when talking about other women, the choices they make, and the opinions they have: "Good for her; not for me." Whether you want to keep things buttoned up or be a #sluttymommy, stay at home or continue to kick ass at the office, bottle-feed or breastfeed, dress your kid in hand-me-downs or couture, we can all be the wives and mothers in whatever way serves us the best.

The key is—once again—tapping into the reserve of Boss Bitch strength and clarity that you've been building all along. The more resolve and confidence you have in your choices, the easier it will be to shut out the voices that having nothing to do with (A) Reality, (B) Your life, and (C) Anything positive or productive that you need to pay attention to. So give any hateration a hair toss and tell 'em "I love it when you call me big mama."

GET BITCHY

This exercise is for you whether you're considering getting pregnant, know for a fact that you don't want kids, are already pregnant, or have six kids with one on the way. Regardless of how you choose to Mom, I want you to feel like you can be your truest, most genuine version of you. That's your right! You're entitled to exactly that and no one can take that away, no matter how hard they might try. So the next time some ratchet bitch comes for you, you won't even break a sweat.

I want you to revisit your visualization exercises from chapter 7 for this one. Get comfy and close your eyes. I want you to imagine yourself exactly how you want to be in one year. Is it with your precious three-month-old on your hip? Do you have an adorable belly, whether it's petite or Buddha-style? Are you rocking stilettos and body con dresses? Are you slaying it at work, baby home with the sitter, your partner, or in daycare? Are you traveling the world because you don't have any strings to tie you down? Are you dressing your kids in head-to-toe Gucci with nothing on your schedule but mommy-and-me mani-pedis? Or playing at the park with no pressure to answer work emails because you left behind meetings and conference calls for snack time and naps?

Whatever that looks like for you, I want you to work the steps of manifestation: getting clear AF, making it matter deeply, and imprinting the visual so significantly in your mind that you can feel it in your bones. The beauty of this exercise is that you can use it two ways: to manifest something into existence that isn't already there, or to get even more resolved about how you want things to be. Emphasis on the word YOU, because what you'll notice isn't a part of this exercise is what anyone else has to say about it. OK, maybe you should be on the same page as Baby Daddy or Baby Co-Mama, but otherwise, this has to do with what feels right to you and only you.

EPILOGUE

STEAL THE SHOW

From the time I was little, I knew that I wanted to tell my story. I always loved trying on different characters and getting reactions from people—laughing, crying, feeling all the feels—so I knew that acting would be an ideal path for me. But my real dream was to be on TV *playing myself*. Playing a character always felt like I was hindering a part or parts of myself that I couldn't show because, duh, that wasn't the gig. I wanted to be unedited, unleashed. Well before reality TV was a thing, except for maybe the Kardashians—brilliant bitches that they are—this is what I wanted. So when *Selling Sunset* approached me about being on this little show that no one knew anything about and had no way of anticipating just how big it would be, I thought, *Why the fuck not?* I can be myself but play it up a little bit, have some fun, and push some boundaries to the max. I just knew that if I was going to do it, then I was going to be unapologetically me. I needed to majorly stand out.

In the beginning, I didn't care how I got the screen time, I just want to be remembered. So yeah, maybe I picked a fight or two in the first season to tee myself up for the perfect finale finish and secure a second season. Oops (and you're welcome). Oh, and I definitely showed out in the fiercest outfits. And I did it all with purpose, because I knew that this was my moment to introduce myself to the world. All so I could have a platform to tell my own story. Because as I like to say: If you don't tell it, someone else will. And ownership rights over this chick's life story are not for sale.

When the show aired for the first time on Netflix and blew the fuck up, that's when everything changed. My Instagram handle—which the network told me to secure in order to "work on my platform" because I'd never been on social media before, for real—suddenly had 500,000 people waiting to see what I did, wore, or said next; which eventually turned into millions. Suddenly all those little squares that I did or didn't post (it would drive people crazy when I wouldn't post for a while, but I kind of liked keeping people in suspense—*Where did she go??*) were reaching all these people, and they responded in droves. They told me that they saw themselves in me or that they related with me on a personal level; they asked me questions like *How can I be more confident?* or *How can I work on my personal style?* (Read up, ladies!); and they were dedicating fan pages to me. That's a lot of love! It made me realize that I was meant to share my experiences and tell my story.

My fans say I steal the show on *Selling Sunset*, but what I'm most proud of is how I've stolen the show that is my own life and inspired others to do the same along they way. Yeah, I might have to work with people who are boring, manipulative, fawning, or backstabbing (more tea on this in a moment), but what really matters is that I own my life and that nobody else will ever dim my spotlight. (And speaking of the spotlight, take selfies during the golden hour—that period right after sunrise or right before sunset. You'll look fabulous. I swear by this, and I'll be damned if there is ever an unflattering shadow in any of my perfect posts! But I digress. . .) I've realized that I'm not meant to be an ensemble player, a co-star among 11 others. I'm meant to be *the* star. I recognize my value. I'm so much more than 1 of 11; I'm 1 of 1. We're *all* 1 of 1—I even wish the other girls on the show realized that instead of trying to compete for Alpha status. (We all know who'd win that one.) I'm grateful for these experiences because it's made me realize what I need from my life: to be myself, completely unedited. And that's driven me to new, amazing heights like launching my empire and writing this book—really showing people who I am.

What I've learned from these past few years of *Selling Sunset* has sort of been like a Boss Bitch master class. It combines all the lessons I've talked about in this book—defining my brand so I can be authentically me, never fearing the hustle, never apologizing unnecessarily, never letting a relationship water down the power of this pussycat, and never—I mean never—feeling sorry for myself when I'm down for the count. So it only makes sense that as we wrap both this book and Season 5 of the show, that I share more of those lessons with you.

If your life is a show (and it is, metaphorically speaking), who are your producers? Do they put words in your mouth? Do they hand you a script somebody else wrote? Who's in your cast of characters? Are you the star, or do you let someone else stand front and center? Are the people around you constantly trying to dim your light? If so, maybe you need to get a new cast, a new writer, a new director. That's because you never have to accept anybody else's reality. You don't have to say what others tell you to say, or wear what others tell you to wear, or be what others tell you that you need to be. You say what you want and wear what you want and be exactly who you are, no matter what, and the show that is *your life* will never, ever get canceled.

These days, I'm living by that idea because I'm finally fully living my truth. For so long I lived in the blank space of the Christine that the writers and producers of the show wanted me to be. They didn't show who I was as a person—they edited and filtered and warped things so much that I became a character. Not even, a *caricature*. That's where my disappointment with the show took root, even as I was spreading my wings more than ever thanks to my newfound platform. Because even though I was able to connect with and touch so many people thanks to all the exposure, I was having to deal with people coming at me because they believed the Christine on *Selling Sunset* was the Christine in real life. It made me want to scream UM WHAT?! It's TV, people!

I once got fired (and then rehired) by the production company because I was pointing out in interviews all the things that had been manipulated—from our dialogue, to our relationships, to our actual listings. Our clients didn't want their houses turned into sets, and most of them didn't want to get involved with the shit show that is reality TV. So the producers would feed us listings, especially the new girls. Fans wanted to know what the real deal was, and these big glossy lips of mine weren't about to keep any secrets. Of course, by the next season we all had to sign NDAs, you know, to preserve the "magic curtain" and all that bullshit. So, when people asked me if things "really happened that way"—which they so obviously didn't—I couldn't say otherwise. And I started to suffer because of it. When people met me in real life or wrote articles about me, it was about Christine Quinn, star of *Selling Sunset*, not Christine Quinn, human being. I was the bitch, the ice queen, the this, the that—and yeah, some of that was a carefully curated alter ego, and some of that isn't so far from the truth (tbh), but a lot of it was a result of the real pieces of me landing on the cutting-room floor. The same thing was happening to everyone else, too—we were told that it would be a show about our work, about real estate, but little did we know, the show was really about the drama, most of which was manufactured to make good television. I'd text the producer and say, "Listen, I have three fucking houses right now that we can film in; I have two listings that are signed—why are you not showing my real estate?" Because they didn't want to. I was never meant to be a real estate prodigy on the show; I was meant to be the villain.

These last two seasons were a real moment of truth for me. I couldn't show up without a pit in my stomach about how they were going to butcher this or manipulate that. And unfortunately, I was right to feel that way. My life was diced up and rearranged to tell the show's story, not mine. That scene in Season 4 where I'm doing yoga inversions while chatting with Davina? They placed it to look like I was doing it *after* I gave birth—as if to imply that I had bounced back really quickly. (And leading some to say a little too quickly.) But I was still pregnant! They just didn't show my bump. So I was left with the backlash of false pregnancy accusations, which were some of the most overwhelmingly hurtful comments I'd ever received. I was also feeling lonelier than ever because it was hard to tell if the people surrounding me were legit friends of mine or just needed something from me. They say it's lonely at the top, and in my former life I would have said, "Yeah, whatever, in your fucking private jet or yacht or whatever; I feel so bad for you," but now I get it. I've also watched the people around me on the show change. That's the one thing no one could ever say about me: *The show changed her.* But I've watched my relationships with some of my castmates explode or fade into the background because I don't even recognize them anymore.

Now, a few seasons in, in order to tell my real story, to *be* more real, it meant taking a huge swing. When you watch Seasons 4 and 5, you'll see a very different Christine. Yeah, there's plenty of me being a total boss and calling out bullshit and unnecessary drama when I see it, but you'll see my softer side, too, crying more and being vulnerable. It goes back to a struggle I always have between my Libra desire to be a rock and a nurturer and my supreme ego's drive to dominate. I want to be uplifting and powerful—the same Christine you know and love—but also have to be able to put down my sword sometimes. It's a back-and-forth that can really wear on me, and especially in Season 4, it was all put into perspective. Because what people won't realize from watching the show is that just one week before filming, I almost died.

A lot comes into clearer focus when you experience potentially life-ending trauma—especially wanting nothing to do with catty noise. For me, it was giving birth to my son. I'll get into it, but let me back up by saying that even pregnancy wasn't easy for me. I didn't start showing until I was six months pregnant, so I really missed out on all the fun, fluffy things that I thought would come with having a baby like taking sweet pics with my growing belly. And by the time I was eight months pregnant, instead of staying home with my feet up and decorating the nursery, I was shooting the show. We filmed Season 4 in roughly *one month*. Watching it you'd think months and months had gone by, but no, I'd be working ten-hour days while about to pop. And then there was the birth itself, which let's just say was far less scripted than any reality TV show you've seen but double the drama.

I was a month away from my due date and had started having contractions, which didn't feel quite right. I told my doctor and her response was "Don't be silly; you're still a month out." I knew that was kind of a weird thing to say, but it was my first time being pregnant, so I didn't think anything of it. That night I was on the red carpet for the MTV Awards because I was presenting and also nominated (for Best Fight with Chrishell—I never do anything half-assed!). I was standing there on the carpet feeling sooo not right, with mystery liquid soaking through my panties even though I had tissues crammed in there, and the cramps. The cramps. When I got home, I texted my doctor again, and she said, "Text me in the morning, blah blah blah, everything's fine." The next day I went to work, and I'll never forget it—Jason made a dumb joke like "Your water's not going to break here in the office, is it? You're not going to give birth here, are you?" Well, I went home from filming that night, and thirty minutes later, this circus balloon pops between my legs. I kept waiting for the gush of fluid to stop, but it didn't. It was just coming and coming, and then the contractions kicked in, fast and furious. At this point I still had in my head an image of what the birth would be like—I could hear my doula telling me in her soft voice about how we're going to count between contractions, drive nice and slowly to the hospital, and then set up some candles in the hospital room. Instead, we were rushing movie-style to the hospital, running red lights, me screaming in pain in the back seat with nothing but a towel wrapped around my waist because I couldn't get pants on thanks to the constant gush from between my legs. And the whole time I'm thinking, *No no no no, this is not how it's supposed to happen. I don't even have a crib yet! I'm not even an adult yet!*

My entire experience at the hospital was a blur. From the minute I got there and was wheeled to Labor and Delivery, everything was a flash of frantic comings and goings. *She's in labor! She's having a baby right now! She's dilated eight centimeters, now it's nine! You have to push! The baby's not coming; get the vacuum, get the vacuum! No time for an epidural. Mom and baby's heart rates are dropping; we need an emergency C-section let's go let's go.* And I'm just like, *Where are my fucking candles?* The entire time, the baby and I were in and out of being stable; at one point, Christian was told to leave because he "wouldn't want to see this." They had to sew me up so quickly that they had to pass me through an X-ray machine to make sure none of their instruments had been left inside me, because they didn't have a spare second to count the tools. My doctor didn't even make it in time for the last stitch. All of that took only twenty-two minutes.

When I came to, I was dazed and confused. I didn't know where I was, and I didn't know where my baby was. I didn't even know if he made it. And I was in so. Much. Pain. When I could finally see my baby—Christian, named after my rock of a husband—holding him was intensely painful. The clash of hormones left me with a nasty case of postpartum depression, which was only made worse by pretty much every post on the *Daily Mail* saying I faked my pregnancy and hired a surrogate. Talk about twisting the fucking knife. But the real kick in the cooch? I was back to filming a week later. A week. Seven days. I had barely healed, nor did I have the emotional capacity to deal with my ruthless castmates.

So yeah, back on set it didn't feel right to go back to pretending that everything was fine. Or that I didn't have any emotions beyond "frosty bitch" and "ballbuster." The girls would be coming after me for some stupid reason or another, and I'd just be like *I cannot. I literally almost died on an operating table, so your problems are null and void for me.* My hope was that I'd be so much more relatable to people. And that by keeping it 100 percent real, people would see the cruelty of the other women, their nasty ways. It may not have always been what they wanted to hear, but I could sleep at night because I was being true to myself.

Meanwhile, back in real life, I was being more honest, too. I was using my platform to connect with people on a level I never had before, opening up about my traumatic birth experience and my struggle with postpartum depression. I figured if I was lamenting not having the "picture perfect" birth experience—like there even is such a thing! People, please stop pretending there is!!—then many of my followers were, too. And sure enough, they reached out with heartfelt gratitude and support.

It still hurts sometimes that the women I was supposed to be friends with on the show could be so cold. Sure, they sent me baby gifts after Christian was born, but it was more like "My assistant needs your address"/ good optics kind of thing. The best gift would have been to be nice to me. Maybe? Just maybe? Let this be a lesson to you, too—your costars in your life movie matter. If that spotlight just happens to shine a little brighter on you, they should be cheering the loudest for you, not trying to block your moment. I never realized what a number jealousy can do on people. My husband put it so well: Me and my castmates have all been given the same opportunity and platform; we were seven people at the ready-set-go line waiting to run the same race. I just happened to Usain Bolt my way around that track. I didn't do that by pushing anyone down or tying anyone's shoelaces together; I did it by being genuinely me. So it came as such a shock when the response was anything but positive. Especially because I always want people to win. If you're my friend, I'm going to be your biggest hype woman. But insecurity is a tricky bitch.

* * *

Its also made me realize how important it is to me to be the main narrator of my story—the truest possible version. The show helped me build my platform and connect with a huge audience. But would I rather be with my family, with my baby, doing yoga, reading, traveling, swimming? Doing all the things that get my mind right? I'm an order-room-service-and-chill kind of girl—I swear I'm low-maintenance . . . ish. I really do value the small things, and that's what fills me up.

I may not totally know where I'm going from here, but what I'm certain of is that whatever I do will be mine, mine, mine. I want to go forward living a non-edited life, not being held back by storylines that someone else is writing for me. I'm going to opt out of things that don't make me feel good and lean *alllll* the way into the things that do. I'm going to listen to the voice inside of me that knows what's up (ESPECIALLY if I think I'm going into labor!) and shut out the ones that only want to bring me down. You know why? Because that's what a Boss Bitch does.

Now that you've read this book, (hopefully) learned from my mistakes, and (more hopefully) been inspired by my successes, it's time to not only write your story but also tell the fuck out of it. We just spent, what, two hundred pages getting a handle on who you are and what you want; so now is the time for you to go out and make it happen. As you saw in my story, it won't magically unfold overnight. Hell, it may not come together for five or ten years. But that doesn't mean that every damn day doesn't count. Every morning that you wake up and get resolved about what kind of bitch that you want to be and own it is a tally in the right column and puts all the amazing, shoot-for-the-stars possibilities available to you in motion. Right fucking now is when you create your own show. Are you going to let someone else write the dialogue, control the narrative, edit out your favorite bits, and otherwise Frankenstein the shit out of your life? No! You're going to produce it, direct it, edit it, and hopefully promote it, too.

I want you to remember this when you go about your life—pay attention to people, feelings, and circumstances that influence your storyline. Do they make it juicy and binge-worthy or too cringe to watch? Are there influences other than your own drives and desires calling the shots about the narrative of your life? Are you only getting scenes that limit you to one dimension of your life? What about your costars—are they supportive when the spotlight shines brightest on you, or are they the first to throw daggers as soon as you turn your back? And then there's the main character—does she look, dress, move, and act the way you want to be putting yourself out there? If you turned on the TV tomorrow and watched an old episode of your life, would you be unhappy with what it looked like, or would you eat up every minute over a big-ass bowl of popcorn?

Call me over-the-top all you want—it certainly wouldn't be the first time—but I want you to consider living your life as though it really could be the next huge Netflix series. Because when you do that, and you nail it, then you'll know that you're really calling all the shots and living in true alignment with your highest self. Plus, I don't know about you, but I love the idea of all of us Boss Bs out there, killing the game, on-screen or not. And along the way, I'm going to do my damnedest to encourage you, prop you up, and cheer you on. That's the inspiration that keeps me passionate about my growing empire. So even though *Selling Sunset* may have wrapped, you definitely haven't seen the last of me. Stay tuned, bitches!

Xoxo,
Christine

Editor: Holly Dolce
Designer: Jack Frischer
Managing Editor: Annalea Manalili
Production Manager: Anet Sirna-Bruder

Library of Congress Control Number: 2021946839

ISBN: 978-1-4197-6094-5
eISBN: 978-1-64700-635-8

Printed and bound in the United States

10 9 8 7 6 5 4 3 2 1

Abrams Image books are available at special discounts when purchased in quantity for premiums and promotions as well as fundraising or educational use. Special editions can also be created to specification. For details, contact specialsales@abramsbooks.com or the address below.

ABRAMS The Art of Books
195 Broadway, New York, NY 10007
abramsbooks.com